"Where you find a healthy church, I bet you'll find flourishing deacons. Bob Thune's book will help you train and deploy these vital servants in your church. I'm always grateful for how Bob combines practical advice with thoughtful reflections on the work of the gospel in our hearts."

Collin Hansen, Editor in Chief and Vice President for Content, The Gospel Coalition; author of *Timothy Keller: His Intellectual and Spiritual Formation*

"A companion to his outstanding book, *Gospel Eldership*, Bob Thune's *Gospel Training for Deacons* is the best resource I know of for identifying and preparing deacons for their service in the local church. It begins with the assumption that Jesus is the quintessential servant leader and is the meaning, model, and means for all leadership in the body of Christ. Because of the crisis of leadership in our culture everywhere, I envision using this book to help disciple servant leaders for callings even beyond the local church."

Scotty Smith, Pastor Emeritus, Christ Community Church, Franklin, TN; teacher in residence, West End Community Church, Nashville, TN

"Bob Thune has been a pastor and church leader for many years—he knows that deacons are a vital part of a healthy, sound church. Whether you are a church leader, someone interested in becoming a deacon, or simply a church member wanting to better understand what a deacon does, this book is a tremendous resource."

Courtney Doctor, Director of Women's Initiatives, The Gospel Coalition; Bible teacher; author of *From Garden to Glory* and *In View of God's Mercies*

"The office of deacon is one of the most significant and yet overlooked roles in the church. In this book, Bob Thune not only casts a biblical vision for the office of deacon, but he also guides readers through a process that cultivates the character befitting the office. Our church has used *Gospel Eldership* for years and I can't wait to use *Gospel Training for Deacons*."

Jeremy Treat, Pastor for Preaching and Vision, Reality LA, Los Angeles, CA; adjunct professor of theology, Biola University; author of *Seek First*

GOSPEL TRAINING FOR DEACONS

GOSPEL TRAINING FOR DEACONS

EQUIPPING SERVANT LEADERS

Robert H. Thune

New Growth Press, Greensboro, NC 27401

Emphasis in Scripture added by author.

Cover Design: Faceout Books, faceoutstudio.com
Interior Layout and Typesetting: Lisa Parnell, lparnellbookservices.com

ISBN: 978-1-64507-437-3 (paperback)
ISBN: 978-1-64507-438-0 (ebook)

Printed in India

29 28 27 26 25   2 3 4 5 6

CONTENTS

INTRODUCTION: WHAT IS A DEACON?

Leadership is a basic human reality. When kids play football on the playground, someone picks the teams. When volunteers get together to clean up a neighborhood park, someone organizes the initiative. When friends get together for a book club, someone chooses the book and plans the discussion. Every human community has some form of leadership.

Right now you're reading a resource on church leadership. Based on that fact, I can deduce that you have some interest in church leadership, or perhaps one of the leaders in your church sees leadership potential in you. What I don't know are your current convictions about church leadership, your past experiences with church leadership, or your present context. So let's start with a basic observation we can all agree on:

Every church has leaders.

Starting from that universal reality, the real question we need to ask is *What* ***kind*** *of leaders should the church have?* Did God intend his church to be led by just anyone? Or did he give some outline, some matrix, some set of instructions for church leadership?

Thankfully, God has answered these questions for us in his Word to his people—the Bible. In the book of Acts, we learn that the apostles appointed **elders** to lead the churches: "And when they had appointed *elders* for them in every church, with prayer and fasting they committed them to the Lord in whom they had believed" (Acts 14:23). We also see the apostles entrusting the practical needs of the church to a **second group** of leaders:

> And the twelve summoned the full number of the disciples and said, "It is not right that we should give up preaching the

> word of God to serve tables. Therefore, brothers, pick out from among you seven men of good repute, full of the Spirit and of wisdom, whom we will appoint to this duty. But we will devote ourselves to prayer and to the ministry of the word." (Acts 6:2–4)

The apostles seemed to envision two distinct ministries within the church: pastoral and practical. Some leaders were to devote themselves to "prayer and the ministry of the word." Other leaders were to focus on meeting practical needs. The offices of elder and deacon correspond to these two types of ministry. Though elders and deacons aren't specifically mentioned in Acts 6, the basic differentiation between pastoral and practical ministry lays a foundation that the rest of the New Testament will build upon.

The goal of this resource is to prepare people for practical ministry in the office of deacon (those interested in learning about elders can consult my companion resource, *Gospel Eldership*). But first, let's take a look at how the Bible defines a deacon.

WHAT IS A DEACON?

A deacon is a servant

The Greek term translated "deacon" is *diakonos*, meaning "servant." This word appears twenty-nine times in the New Testament. Related terms are the verb *diakoneo* ("to serve," thirty-six times in the NT) and the noun *diakonia* ("service, ministry, office," thirty-three times in the NT). "The original frame of reference for the use of the entire word group . . . was that of table service."[1] From the original meaning that describes a "waiter," the term developed a more general sense to connote "one who serves."

Consider the following New Testament references:

- John 2:9 (NIV): "The master of the banquet tasted the water that had been turned into wine. He did not realize where it had come from, though the servants [*diakonoi*] who had drawn the water knew."

- Luke 22:25–27 (NIV): "The kings of the Gentiles lord it over them. . . . But you are not to be like that. Instead, the greatest among you should be like the youngest, and the one who rules like the one who serves [*diakonon*]. . . . I am among you as one who serves [*diakonon*]."
- John 12:26 (NIV): "Whoever serves [*diakone*] me must follow me; and where I am, my servant [*diakonos*] also will be. My Father will honor the one who serves [*diakone*] me."
- Ephesians 3:7 (NIV): "I became a servant [*diakonos*] of this gospel by the gift of God's grace given to me through the working of his power."

In all of these cases, *diakonos* expresses some aspect of the general term "servant." So a deacon is someone who serves Christ by serving others.

A deacon is an officeholder

We speak of a president, a governor, or a city council member as an "officeholder." These people are elected to an office, in which they serve for a set period of time. Likewise, the Greek word *diakonos* is sometimes used in a more technical sense to describe the formal office of deacon.[2] This more technical use is found in Philippians 1:1 and 1 Timothy 3:8–13.

- Philippians 1:1: "Paul and Timothy, servants of Christ Jesus, to all the saints in Christ Jesus who are at Philippi, with the **overseers** and **deacons**."
- 1 Timothy 3:8–13: "**Deacons** likewise must be dignified, not double-tongued, not addicted to much wine, not greedy for dishonest gain. They must hold the mystery of the faith with a clear conscience. And let them also be tested first; then let them serve as **deacons** if they prove themselves blameless. Their wives [literally "the women"] likewise must be dignified, not slanderers,

> but sober-minded, faithful in all things. Let **deacons** each be the husband of one wife, managing their children and their own households well. For those who serve well as **deacons** gain a good standing for themselves and also great confidence in the faith that is in Christ Jesus."

So the word *diakonos* has both a broader meaning (*servant*) and a narrower meaning (*deacon*). You might think of it this way: though every deacon is a servant, not every servant is a deacon.

The fact that there are only two clear references to the **office** of deacon in the New Testament has caused some scholars to question whether such an office actually existed. One writer argues that elders and deacons were merely roles within the church, not "definite offices."[3] But in his commentary on Philippians, J. Alec Motyer asserts:

> The impression we receive in the New Testament is of local churches loosely federated under apostolic authority, with each church managing its own affairs under the leadership of overseers (who are also called elders) and deacons. **Deacons were obviously a distinct office**, but we are told nothing about the functions a deacon was meant to fulfill. . . . And if we ask why their representative functions are not more closely defined, then surely the answer is this: ministry arises from the nature and needs of the church, not vice versa.[4]

If a deacon is simply a **role** within the church, then that role can be filled informally as church members use their spiritual gifts to serve the body. But if the word "deacon" denotes an **office** within the church, then a properly organized, biblically functioning church should have both elders and deacons serving officially in their God-ordained capacities.

At least two lines of evidence lead me to conclude that the New Testament mandates the *office* of deacon.

First, in both Philippians 1:1 and 1 Timothy 3, deacons are mentioned in close connection with the elders. There is no doubt that the New

Testament sees eldership as a formal office, instituted by the apostles to provide doctrinal oversight and shepherding care to the churches (see Acts 20:28; 1 Peter 5:1–3; Titus 1:9). Barnabas and Paul "appointed elders . . . in every church" (Acts 14:23). Paul commanded Titus to "appoint elders in every town" on the island of Crete (Titus 1:5). Scripture clearly lists qualifications that every potential elder must meet (Titus 1; 1 Timothy 3). But right after the list of elder criteria in 1 Timothy, we read, "Deacons likewise . . ." The mention of deacons in such tight connection with eldership, and the fact that deacons must meet a list of qualifications to serve, leads most biblical scholars to conclude that deacon, like elder, was a formal office in the New Testament churches.

Second, as we've already seen, Acts 6:1–4 shows an apostolically authorized division of labor that lays the groundwork for the offices of elder and deacon. The word *diakonos* is not used here. The apostles are *not* establishing the formal office of deacon. However, they *are* making a distinction in roles that influences the organization of churches in the later New Testament.

It seems highly probable that as Paul and his companions planted churches, they followed the apostolic pattern in Acts 6. They started by appointing qualified men to fill the most important office: elders who would teach Scripture and guard the integrity of the gospel. They expected those elders to follow the pattern of Acts 6, teaching the Bible, growing the church, and eventually delegating some aspects of ministry to qualified disciples. This explains Paul's emphasis on appointing elders first (Titus 1:5), the sequence of 1 Timothy 3 (elders, then deacons) and the differing requirements for each office. "When the churches were young, Paul appointed overseers, not deacons. But in the more established churches of Philippi (Philippians 1:1) and Ephesus (1 Timothy 3:8–13) there were both overseers and deacons. Perhaps the latter office developed on a church-by-church basis as the size and needs of the church increased."[5]

Because of the strong textual connection between deacons and elders, and because of the echoes of an Acts-6-style division of labor in the churches of the New Testament, I conclude that the New Testament clearly teaches the office of deacon should be a part of the local church. If you're asked to serve as a deacon, you're stepping into a formal office of leadership that bears biblical authority and responsibility.

A deacon is a doer

"Be doers of the word, and not hearers only," exhorts the apostle James (James 1:22). Deacons are to be the church's exemplary doers. From the foregoing biblical discussion, we can discern some of the key differences between the office of elder and the office of deacon:

- *Elders are generally appointed first, then deacons.* The first step in organizing a local church is to appoint qualified men to be elders. This was Paul's consistent practice in New Testament church planting (Acts 14:23; Titus 1:5). Elders were raised up first to guard the gospel and shepherd the flock (Titus 1:9). Deacons were appointed later as practical ministry needs increased.[6]
- *Deacons give elders the freedom to focus on the work of shepherding.* Only one important qualification distinguishes elders from deacons: elders must be "able to teach" (1 Timothy 3:2) and "able to . . . rebuke those who contradict [sound doctrine]" (Titus 1:9). There is no such requirement for deacons. Elders, then, are charged primarily with the theological, spiritual, and moral leadership of the church, focusing especially on the faithful teaching of Scripture. Deacons are charged with the practical leadership of the church under the oversight of the elders. Deacons free the elders to give full attention to shepherding the flock, especially with respect to "prayer and the ministry of the word" (Acts 6:4). Elders serve by leading; deacons lead by serving.
- *Deacons do what's needed.* While the New Testament outlines in copious detail the practical duties of elders,[7] it offers almost no teaching about the specific responsibilities of deacons. Alec Motyer uses the word "flexibility" to describe the ideal trait of a deacon. Just as the apostles delegated practical ministry tasks

> to the seven leaders in Acts 6, so the elders delegate practical ministry duties to deacons as the needs of the church increase. "Deacons . . . are to be honorable and sincere in performing *the duties assigned to them by the presbyters* [elders]," wrote Theodore of Mopsuestia.[8]

Deacons, then, are officers of the church who lead by serving. Here's a simple, specific summary of the role of a deacon, from Providence Church in Austin, Texas, that might be helpful as you think through how deacons might serve in your church:

- **What is a deacon?** An officer of the church, distinct from elders, who embodies God's provision and care for the church.
- **What do deacons do? (generally)** Deacons lead by serving. They possess the qualities outlined in 1 Timothy 3, and they function in roles that allow the elders to give more attention to shepherding the flock, especially with respect to "prayer and the ministry of the word" (Acts 6:1–6).
- **What do deacons do? (specifically at Providence Church)** They help provide credibility and stability to the visible leadership of the church. They perform **general** duties related to the office . . . and they serve in **specific** areas of ministry.
- **Who can be a deacon?** Qualified men and women (according to 1 Timothy 3) who are called by God, examined by the community, trained by church leaders, and installed by the elders.[9]

Your church might summarize the role of deacon slightly different. The specific ways deacons help elders can be different from one church to another, and it's also possible that your church might not ordain women to be deacons. From my study of Scripture and biblical scholarship, I believe that while the Bible teaches that elders should be men, women can and should serve as deacons. Lesson 2 will discuss this question in more detail.

Because they are leaders in the church, deacons help to shape the culture of the church. And because God wants every local church to reflect the beauty and glory of his grace, deacons themselves must be *grounded and rooted in the gospel.* They must lead out of their own need for grace. They must know their own heart idolatry and how the good news of the gospel applies to it. And they must have a sense of "gospel fluency" so that they can effectively apply the gospel to others. Those are the kind of leaders that the church needs and that I'm hoping this book will help to develop.

HOW TO USE THIS RESOURCE

This book can be used in a number of different ways. It's designed to be adaptable for different settings and contexts. But it's written with three primary audiences in mind.

1. Current church leaders who want to deepen their theological understanding and their gospel fluency.
2. Deacons-in-training who are progressing through a season of learning and examination.
3. Christians who are seeking to better understand the Bible's teaching about local church leadership.

From my experience, you'll see the best results when this book is used as a small-group study. Ideally, an elder or deacon should lead a group of emerging leaders through the content. This way, the written material serves as a springboard for the more important work of personal mentorship and spiritual formation. The following is a suggested weekly plan for using the resource in this way:

1. Have each participant read the article and work through the exercise independently during the week.
2. Come together as a group for 90–120 minutes to
   a. Talk through the discussion questions.
   b. Share what you learned in the exercises.
   c. Cultivate honest, transformative relationships with one another.

The focus of this group time is not information, but formation. Therefore, each participant should come ready to share openly and honestly. You don't necessarily need to talk through every single question (though sometimes that's fruitful). Rather, feel free to hone in on whatever aspects of the lesson are most thought-provoking and character-shaping to your particular group.

WHAT TO EXPECT

Expect to be challenged. This resource is not intended to reinforce what you already know, but to reshape and reform your understanding of church leadership. Along the way, you'll be challenged and provoked.

Expect to be surprised. This book is intended to provoke self-discovery and to uncover heart idolatry, sin, and selfishness you may not be aware of. This is a *good* thing because it invites you into deeper partnership and fellowship with the Holy Spirit! But it's also a *surprising* thing because self-awareness has a way of sneaking up on you when you least expect it.

Expect a deeper level of community. If you work through this resource with a small group of leaders, as recommended above, the Holy Spirit will forge strong bonds of fellowship. Be ready to know and be known in ways that go far beyond your current experience.

Expect a deeper love for Christ and his church. As I've written this resource, this is what I've prayed for. I hope this resource awakens a deeper love for Jesus, for his church, and for his already-and-not-yet kingdom.

1
LESSON

SERVANT LEADERSHIP

OBJECTIVE

To examine how Jesus's model of leadership differs from the world's default mode of leadership, and how Jesus makes this sort of leadership possible.

SCRIPTURE READING

- Mark 10:32–45

ARTICLE

When you think of Jesus, do you think of him as the most effective leader who's ever lived?

If Jesus really does "uphold the universe by the word of his power" (Hebrews 1:3); if "by him all things were created" (Colossians 1:16); if in him "are hidden all the treasures of wisdom and knowledge" (Colossians 2:3), then clearly he knows everything about leadership. He knows more than the most successful CEO, the sharpest leadership consultant, the most compelling influencer. What Jesus has to teach us about leadership is life-altering. And "leadership experts" have been rediscovering it for centuries.

THE DEFAULT PARADIGM

Jesus's instructions about leadership stand in stark contrast to the status quo. The world's default model of leadership, practiced over centuries and across cultures, is about ***being served***. There's a hierarchy, and the leader is at the top. The followers serve the will of the leader, fulfill the desires of the leader, and further the interests of the leader. When God's people asked for a king, he warned them about the reality of this kind of leadership.

> "These will be the ways of the king who will reign over you: he will take your sons and appoint them to his chariots and to be his horsemen and to run before his chariots. . . . He will take your daughters to be perfumers and cooks and bakers. He will take the best of your fields and vineyards and olive orchards and give them to his servants. He will take the tenth of your grain and of your vineyards and give it to his officers and to his servants. He will take your male servants and female servants and the best of your young men and your donkeys, and put them to his work. He will take the tenth of your flocks, and you shall be his slaves." (1 Samuel 8:11–17)

Jesus's disciples were well schooled in this paradigm of leadership. They envisioned Jesus's kingdom as more of the same. And they wanted to make sure they had a place at the top.

> And James and John, the sons of Zebedee, came up to him and said to him, "Teacher, we want you to do for us whatever we ask of you." And he said to them, "What do you want me to do for you?" And they said to him, "Grant us to sit, one at your right hand and one at your left, in your glory." Jesus said to them, "You do not know what you are asking. Are you able to drink the cup that I drink, or to be baptized with the baptism with which I am baptized?" And they said to him, "We are able." And Jesus said to them, "The cup that I drink you will drink, and with the baptism with which I am baptized, you will be baptized, but to sit at my right hand or at my left is not mine to grant, but it is for those for whom it has been prepared." And when the ten heard it, they began to be indignant at James and John. (Mark 10:35–41)

In response to this request, Jesus turned the conventional thinking about leadership on its head. He introduced a whole new paradigm of leadership.

> And Jesus called them to him and said to them, "You know that those who are considered rulers of the Gentiles lord it over them, and their great ones exercise authority over them. But it shall not be so among you. But whoever would be great among you must be your servant, and whoever would be first among you must be slave of all. For even the Son of Man came not to be served but to serve, and to give his life as a ransom for many." (Mark 10:42–45)

Jesus is *prescribing* for his disciples the kind of leadership they ought to practice, and he's also *describing* what he himself has come to do. Jesus expects his followers to be *servant leaders*. And he's come to make them just that. As the Chief Servant, he will give his life as a ransom to deliver his people from selfish leadership and to free them for radical servant leadership.

So how does a "Jesus way of leadership" become a reality in us?

JESUS IS OUR EXAMPLE

First, Jesus is our example. He is the ultimate Servant Leader. He is the one we are to emulate. He is our model, our archetype, our pattern. "If I then, your Lord and Teacher, have washed your feet, you also ought to wash one another's feet. For I have given you an example, that you also should do just as I have done to you" (John 13:14–15).

Following Jesus's example means we jettison our false, flawed, self-advancing concepts of leadership. We embrace servant leadership as good, true, and beautiful. And then we *decide* to pursue it. We commit to it. We apprentice ourselves to Jesus and resolve that we will become servant leaders.

JESUS IS OUR SUBSTITUTE

Once we decide to follow Jesus's path of servant leadership, we begin to come face-to-face with the selfishness and sinfulness deep within us. Jesus's way of leading is impossible! It is contrary to the bent of our hearts. We want power. We want control. We want comfort, ease, and convenience. We want to be liked, needed, appreciated. We want to do what works for us. We want to be served rather than to serve.

This is why the gospel is foundational to Christian leadership! To flawed and fallen leaders, the gospel proclaims: "Rejoice! Jesus has come to redeem you." Jesus is not just our *model*; he is our *mediator*. The Son of Man came to serve selfish, greedy, flawed leaders. He died for us so that we might live for him. Our hope is not in our excellent servant leadership; our hope is in Jesus's perfect servanthood toward those who acknowledge their lack and their need.

JESUS IS OUR POWER

When weak leaders depend on a strong Christ, he does not just forgive their sins; he empowers them with his renewing grace. The Bible uses the metaphor of "pouring" to describe how generously God gives his Holy Spirit to his people through Jesus: "He saved us . . . by the washing of regeneration and renewal of the Holy Spirit, *whom he poured out on us richly* through Jesus Christ our Savior" (Titus 3:5–6). Whatever you lack, the Spirit has. Whatever you need, the Spirit can provide.

Paradoxically, then, the most servant-hearted leaders are those who are most aware of their struggles with servanthood. Why? Because these leaders are constantly going to Christ for fresh strength. They are constantly depending on the Spirit. They are constantly in lack, constantly in need, and therefore constantly experiencing God's renewing grace. The late seminary professor and pastor Jack Miller summarized the good news of the gospel using two phrases:[1]

- ***Cheer up! You're worse than you think!*** Your failures and flaws are even deeper than you know. Your capacity for servant leadership is smaller than you imagine. Your selfishness is stronger than you've realized. But . . .

- ***Cheer up! The gospel is far greater than you can imagine!*** God is not constrained by your limitations! God uses the weak, the flawed, the powerless. God loves to pour out his Spirit on humble leaders who acknowledge their need.

CONCLUSION

Gospel leadership is servant leadership; and servant leadership drives us back to the gospel. We cannot be the servant leaders Jesus commands us to be without believing the good news of the gospel. Likewise, we cannot believe the gospel without being moved toward greater servanthood. This cycle of renewal brings life and joy and fruitfulness to our leadership.

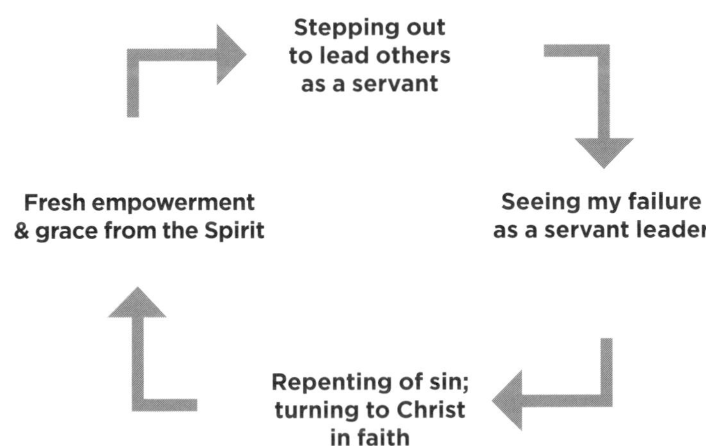

DISCUSSION QUESTIONS

1. What is it about leadership that attracts you? Why do you want to be a leader?

2. What about "the Jesus way of leadership" do you find compelling?

3. Have you made a conscious, intentional commitment to embrace servant leadership? If so, when? If not, are you ready to do that now?

4. What further questions does this lesson raise for you?

1

EXERCISE

SELF-INTERESTED LEADERSHIP

Begin this exercise by taking 3–5 minutes to pause and pray, asking the Holy Spirit to reveal truth and shine his light into your soul: "Search me, O God, and know my heart! Try me and know my thoughts!" (Psalm 139:23).

Next:

Imagine yourself walking into a room full of people from your church. Some of them you know pretty well; others you don't know well at all. You've been asked to lead the gathering—perhaps it's a small-group discussion, or a leadership meeting, or a volunteer training. Someone introduces you, saying: "Everyone, this is ___; he/she is one of our new deacons here at ___ Church." Everyone turns to give you their attention.

In that moment, what do you desire from these people? Perhaps you want them to respect you. Perhaps you want them to think you're smart, or funny, or relatable. Perhaps you want them to treat you no differently than anyone else—and even ***that*** reveals a longing for something.

This exercise is designed to shed light on the desires we carry with us into any moment of leadership, and the subtle self-interest they reveal.

As you imagine the scenario above, what "asks" are you (implicitly) making of the room?

Here are some possible answers:

- Please listen to me
- Please respect me
- Please respond to me
- Please approve of me
- Please affirm me
- Please notice me
- Please don't notice me
- Please take me seriously
- Please don't take me so seriously
- Something else? Write it here: ____________________

____

How does that "ask" reveal what you're seeking in leadership?

I want/need people to:

James and John ***loved*** Jesus. They were part of his inner circle of disciples. They wanted to see his kingdom advance and his purposes flourish. At the same time, they had their own desires and longings they were hoping to fulfill. In what ways are you like them? What desires and longings are you hoping to fulfill?

Now, let's take our eyes off ourselves and look to Jesus.

Jesus Is Our Example: How do you see Jesus modeling a pure, servant-hearted, non-self-interested type of leadership? Write down specific Scriptures or stories that come to mind.

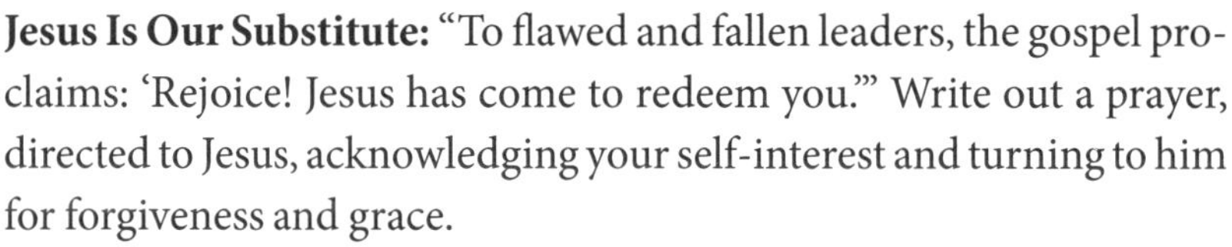

Jesus Is Our Substitute: "To flawed and fallen leaders, the gospel proclaims: 'Rejoice! Jesus has come to redeem you.'" Write out a prayer, directed to Jesus, acknowledging your self-interest and turning to him for forgiveness and grace.

Jesus Is Our Power: "The most servant-hearted leaders are those who are most aware of their struggles with servanthood—these leaders are constantly going to Christ for fresh strength. They are constantly depending on the Spirit." How do you need to go to Christ for fresh strength? What do you need from the Holy Spirit, right now, in order to become the kind of leader God wants you to be?

Pray and seek him now.

2

LESSON

BIBLICAL QUALIFICATIONS FOR DEACONS

OBJECTIVE

To consider the scriptural qualifications for those who hold the office of deacon.

SCRIPTURE READING

- 1 Timothy 3:1–13

ARTICLE

Recently, while waiting at the dentist's office, I noticed an odd similarity between my dentist, physical therapist, and auto mechanic. In all three businesses, certificates are posted on the wall in the waiting area. The dentist has framed his professional credentials for all to see. The physical therapist has posted her state-approved license to practice medicine. And the mechanic has displayed his certification from the automotive service industry.

In each of these fields, qualifications matter. When we have trouble with our teeth, bodies, or cars, we want to turn to people who know what they're doing—and who have the credentials to prove it. We want to entrust ourselves to people who are qualified.

In a similar way, qualifications matter for church leadership. God protects and guards his church by giving clear guidelines for who can serve as an elder or deacon. Only those who meet the biblical criteria are fit for the office.

EXCLUSIVE?

Isn't it exclusive to say that only **certain** people can serve as deacons?

Yes, it is. But this is one of those places where exclusivity is *good*. If the medical board in your state said that only white men could serve as doctors, you'd rightly protest that sort of exclusivity. But when they say that only people with a medical degree can serve as doctors, you celebrate it. Why? Because being a medical doctor requires a certain sort of training, and we want every doctor to have that training! We don't want cut-rate medical impostors doing surgery out of pickup trucks. We want standards and testing and certification.

Likewise, qualifications for elders and deacons are a safeguard for both the leaders and the people. They protect the church against dishonest, defective, or domineering leaders. And they help leaders overcome their own insecurity, uncertainty, and self-concern. Knowing that you've been examined and tested against biblical criteria leads to "great confidence in the faith that is in Christ Jesus" (1 Timothy 3:13). Saying that deacons must be qualified is like saying that doctors must be certified: it's good for the patient, good for the doctor, and good for society as a whole.

DEACON QUALIFICATIONS

Below are the biblical qualifications for deacons, as found in 1 Timothy 3:8–13 (original Greek terms are bracketed in italics). In this lesson, we'll consider a few questions the text raises, and then explore each qualification.

> Deacons likewise must be dignified [*semnous*], not double-tongued [*dilogous*], not addicted to much wine, not greedy for dishonest gain [*aischrokerdeis*]. They must hold the mystery of the faith with a clear conscience [*syneidesei*]. And let them also be tested [*dokimazesthoson*] first; then let them serve as deacons if they prove themselves blameless [*anenkletoi*]. Their wives [*gynaikas*, Lit. "The women"] likewise

> must be dignified [*semnas*], not slanderers [*diabolous*], but sober-minded [*nephalious*], faithful [*pistas*] in all things. Let deacons each be the husband of one wife, managing their children and their own households well. For those who serve well as deacons gain a good standing for themselves and also great confidence in the faith that is in Christ Jesus.

Wait . . . can only men be deacons?

The reference to "their wives" and the requirement that a deacon be "the husband of one wife" seems to imply that deacons are men. But as noted, the Greek word used in verse 11 can be translated as "wives" or "women." So is the text speaking of *the wife of a deacon* or of *a female deacon*? Can women serve as deacons?

Just prior to these verses, we find the qualifications for elders (1 Timothy 3:1–7), which include no requirement for an elder's wife. Since eldership is the higher office in the church, it would be strange for God to require something of deacons' wives that he does not require of elders' wives. And though appeals to history are secondary to biblical exegesis, "it is indisputable . . . that an order of deaconesses did quickly arise in the church," observes historian Hermann W. Beyer.[1] John Chrysostom, one of the great church fathers of the fourth century (c. 349–407), understood 1 Timothy 3:11 to refer to "those who hold the rank of deaconesses."[2] In cultures which were strongly patriarchal, the early leaders of the church saw the appointment of deaconesses as a sound and scriptural practice.

Note what *The Oxford Dictionary of the Christian Church* records about the early church's practice:

> The deaconess devoted herself to the care of the sick and the poor of her sex; she was present at interviews of women with bishops, priests, or deacons; instructed women catechumens; and kept order in the women's part of the church. Her most important function was the assistance at the baptism of

> women . . . which, for reasons of propriety . . . could not be performed by the [male] deacons.[3]

In light of this biblical and historical evidence, I conclude that women can and should serve as deacons. Though some differ on this point, I find the witness of early church history and the exegetical evidence in 1 Timothy 3 to favor both men and women serving in the diaconal office.

How should deacons be tested?

First Timothy 3:10 demands that deacons "be tested first; then let them serve as deacons if they prove themselves blameless." What is this "testing" to look like? And who should oversee it?

The natural conclusion, both from the flow of the passage and the consistent witness of history, is that elders should oversee the testing and examination of deacons. In the Book of Common Prayer (the pastoral guide of the Anglican Church), the service for the ordination of a deacon envisions candidates being presented before the presiding bishop, who examines them and ordains them into the office. The ordination vow includes a promise to "reverently obey your Bishop and other Ministers who have charge and authority over you." Though such a charge may feel rather formal and hierarchical to modern sensibilities, it reflects the uniform understanding of the church throughout history. Deacons serve under the authority of elders/pastors, assisting them in carrying out the practical duties of ministry.

Deacons should be examined in both character ("dignified, not double-tongued, not addicted to much wine, not greedy for dishonest gain") and confession ("hold[ing] the mystery of the faith with a clear conscience"). While deacons aren't required, as elders are, to "give instruction in sound doctrine" (Titus 1:9), they do need to have a firm grasp of the gospel and of basic Christian orthodoxy. No one should be installed as a deacon without being tested and proven in both character and confession. At the Council of Chalcedon in AD 451, the minimum age for a deacon was fixed at forty. Though this is not a scriptural requirement, it does show that the early church expected age and maturity to go together. Qualifying as a deacon requires a depth of character that doesn't grow overnight.

The qualifications: a closer look

Reflecting on each word and phrase in the list of qualifications gives a fuller picture of what a faithful deacon looks like:

- *Dignified*: honorable, noble, worthy of respect; the kind of people whom younger Christians should seek to emulate.
- *Not double-tongued*: honest and truthful; straightforward. In Greek this phrase has the idea of not "speaking out of both sides of your mouth" or "thinking one thing but saying another."
- *Not addicted to much wine*: no addictions; self-controlled in habits.
- *Not greedy for dishonest gain*: not "in it for the money"—they serve because they love God, not because they hope to get paid.
- *Must hold the mystery of the faith with a clear conscience*: orthodox in belief; morally sensitive and attuned to the voice of conscience; no discrepancy between what they profess and how they live.
- *Must first be tested*: proved faithful over time; stand up under examination.
- Additional requirements for female deacons:
  - » *Dignified*: honorable, noble, worthy of respect; women whom younger Christians would want to emulate.
  - » *Not slanderers*: they don't participate in gossip or "talking trash" about others.
  - » *Sober-minded*: restrained, self-controlled; don't give vent to their passions and emotions.
  - » *Faithful in all*: dependable, reliable, trustworthy in all responsibilities

- Additional requirements for married male deacons:
  - » *A one-woman man*: faithful to wife; sexually pure.
  - » *Manages his children and household well*: leads, manages, and provides for his family; children respect and obey their father.

APPLYING THE GOSPEL

Looking at a list of qualifications like this, most people have one of two responses. Some presume they're already qualified; others assume they'll never be qualified. Both responses need to be interrogated by the gospel.

On the one hand, these ***are*** qualifications. That means it IS possible to achieve them! There are people in the church who meet these standards. Perhaps you are one of them. In that case, your posture of heart makes all the difference.

Consider the apostle Paul. He had a stellar résumé: "Circumcised on the eighth day, of the people of Israel, of the tribe of Benjamin, a Hebrew of Hebrews; as to the law, a Pharisee; as to zeal, a persecutor of the church; as to righteousness under the law, blameless" (Philippians 3:5–6). Yet he assessed himself as the "foremost" of sinners (1 Timothy 1:15) and "the least of the apostles" (1 Corinthians 15:9). Paul understood that "by the grace of God I am what I am" (1 Corinthians 15:10). Whatever wisdom, maturity, and integrity he had was a gift of God's grace.

If you do meet the biblical qualifications of a deacon, it's evidence of God's grace in your life. So check your heart. Do you feel a deep sense of humility, gratitude, and joy in God's kindness to you? Do you thank him for the maturity he's granted you, and the growth he's given you? Do you repent quickly when you see presumption, pride, or self-reliance? Are you open to others' feedback about your sins and failings? Take an honest look within. Talk with God about what you find there.

Perhaps you don't yet meet these qualifications. In that case, you're not yet ready to serve as a deacon. That's not shameful, sad, or stifling; it's *grace*. God is inviting you into deeper growth and transformation. You *can* meet these qualifications, by grace, over time. The fact that you don't meet them now doesn't mean you *won't* meet them. It means that God loves you enough to call you to deeper change, and he loves his church enough to hold its leaders to a high standard. Look squarely at the places where you need further growth. Talk with God and others about them.

Of course, examining your life against these qualifications isn't something you do alone; it's something that happens in community. Ideally, the elders or congregation of your local church will invite you into a process of training and testing. Perhaps this study is part of that process. For the sake of your own soul, it's important not to treat the process as a pass/fail exam. You aren't validated as a Christian by becoming a deacon. By applying the gospel to your own heart along the way, you can learn to say with Paul: "I have learned in whatever situation I am to be content" (Philippians 4:11). If I serve as a deacon, I'm content; if I don't serve as a deacon, I'm equally content. "In any and every circumstance . . . I can do all things through him who strengthens me" (Philippians 4:12–13).

CONCLUSION

Character change takes time. It may take years of steady growth to meet the biblical qualifications for deacons. Don't get impatient. The Lord is not "over there," waiting for you to hurry up and change. He's right here, with you. He's dwelling in you by his Spirit—convicting you of sin, empowering your repentance and faith, and making you more like his Son. Because Jesus loves you, he's more committed than you are to changing you. And because he loves his church, he's committed to making sure it has the best and most qualified leaders. So enjoy the journey. And enjoy *him* in the midst of the journey.

DISCUSSION QUESTIONS

1. Identify some other vocations where qualifications really matter. What are the dangers of unqualified people in these vocations? What are the dangers of unqualified leaders in the church?

2. Share about a time when you experienced poor leadership in a church. (Try to keep this general and share without gossiping or naming specific individuals or churches.) What did you learn through that experience?

3. Look through the list of deacon qualifications. Which one surprises you the most? Why?

4. What further questions does this lesson raise for you?

2
EXERCISE

CHANGE PROJECT, PART 1

Over the next few exercises, we're going to get serious about change. I'm going to invite you to identify an area of needed change in your life—it could be a sin that needs to be put to death, or a virtue that needs to be brought to life, or a negative emotion that needs to be transformed, or an area of unbelief that needs to be replaced with vibrant faith. Then you are going to work on that area deliberately, over time, by applying the good news of the gospel in a deep and focused way.

This may be the first time you've asked questions this deep or focused this intently on a specific area. Enjoy it! Applying the gospel in this way will pay dividends for years to come. As you do this work in yourself, you'll understand better how to help others change, and that, after all, is what Christian ministry is all about.

A BRIEF THEOLOGY OF CHANGE

Change in the Christian life is both critical and progressive. On one hand, faith in Jesus changes us immediately and radically (see 2 Corinthians 5:17). On the other hand, God's grace continues to change us over time (see Ephesians 4:17–32). We are engaged in a lifelong process of sanctification.

The basic message of Jesus is to "repent and believe" (Mark 1:14–15). So what do we DO in order to change? We repent and believe. Repentance and faith are the basic "steps" of sanctification, the simple means by which we are changed. In repentance, we "put off your old self, which belongs to your former manner of life and is corrupt through deceitful desires" (Ephesians 4:22). In faith, we "put on the new self, created after the likeness of God in true righteousness and holiness" (Ephesians 4:24).

Another parallel image for thinking about change is "uprooting the bad tree" and "cultivating the good tree" (see Luke 6:43–45). By attending to the "bad fruit" in our lives, we can see the places where the root is unhealthy. The fruit in our life changes through changing the root—applying the gospel, in repentance and faith, to the idolatry and unbelief of the heart. In this way, the bad fruit of sin and selfishness is replaced by the good fruit of the Spirit (Galatians 5:22–24).

IDENTIFY THE BAD FRUIT

So let's get to work. The first step in the process is to identify some area of "bad fruit" in your life that you want to change, by God's grace. Pause for a moment and pray. Invite the Holy Spirit to bring conviction and illumination. Discern where God is calling you to growth. Here are some ideas to consider:

- The qualifications of a deacon in 1 Timothy 3:8–13
- A negative behavior: lying, lust, impatience, addiction, over-working, talking too much, etc.
- A negative emotion: anger, anxiety, greed, envy, discontentment, apathy, etc.
- How you're dealing with a current situation in life: a relationship, finances, career, kids, etc.
- A particular fear that hinders your growth: rejection, failure, death, etc.

Write down the area where you want to seek change. Be as specific as possible:

Now, sit back and reflect on your struggle in this area.

- WHEN do you struggle the most with this "bad fruit"? What specific situations or circumstances tend to bring it to the forefront?

- WHO is most affected by your struggle in this area? How is it affecting your relationships?

- HOW have you sought to deal with it so far?

- WHY do you want change in this area?

Now, pause and pray. Thank the Father for his love for you. Thank Jesus for his death in your place. Thank the Holy Spirit for giving you the power to change. We'll continue the journey of gospel change in the next exercise.

LESSON

DEACONS AND ELDERS

OBJECTIVE

To consider the differences between deacons and elders, and how both work together to help the church thrive.

SCRIPTURE READING

- Ephesians 4:4–16

ARTICLE

In the Introduction, we discussed that elders and deacons are the two offices of leadership in the New Testament church. This lesson explores the interplay between these two offices.

But first, we should note a very simple implication of the Bible's teaching: every local church ought to have elders and deacons (or ought to be moving in that direction). This is Jesus's mandate for his church. We are not free to treat it as optional.

Perhaps your church already has an elder-and-deacon structure; perhaps not. Let's briefly explore three alternative models of church leadership that are widely practiced but biblically unsupported.

MODEL #1: THE "ANOINTED LEADER" MODEL

The first faulty model of leadership is the model of the "anointed leader." In churches with this form of leadership, the pastor is seen as "God's man" who has the Holy Spirit's blessing and who practices a solo model of leadership. In these churches, deacons usually function as assistants under the pastor's direction.

Biblically, however, pastors are always spoken of in plurality. For instance, Acts 14:23: "When [Paul and Barnabas] had appointed *elders* for them in every church, with prayer and fasting they committed them to the Lord in whom they had believed." Even the apostles, who sometimes served as "solo pastors" as they launched new churches, raised up elders to serve alongside them as quickly as the Holy Spirit allowed. For this reason, the "anointed leader" model of ministry is not a faithful reflection of the New Testament paradigm.

MODEL #2: THE ECCLESIASTICAL HIERARCHY MODEL

The second faulty model of leadership is the ecclesiastical hierarchy model. In this model there is a hierarchy of leadership, from deacon all the way up to bishop, archbishop, and cardinal. Often a local church's leaders are not shepherds selected from *within* the flock, but outsiders brought in to serve for a season before moving on to serve somewhere else. Additionally, the higher offices of leadership such as bishop and cardinal usually don't pastor a specific flock, but rather serve as "leaders at large."

Again, there are a number of problems with this model biblically. First, the words *bishop* (overseer), *elder*, and *pastor* all refer in Scripture to the same office. There is no biblical justification for using these terms to refer to different levels of leadership. Second, the Bible sees elders and deacons as part of the flock, not separate from it. "Be on guard for yourselves and for all the flock, *among which* the Holy Spirit has made you overseers" (Acts 20:28 NASB95). And third, elders and deacons are seen in Scripture as leaders of *a particular local church*. "To all the saints in Christ Jesus who are at Philippi, with the overseers and deacons," writes Paul in Philippians 1:1. The "ecclesiastical hierarchy" model of ministry does not faithfully reflect the New Testament approach.

MODEL #3: THE CEO/BOARD MODEL

The third faulty model of leadership is the CEO/Board Model. In this model, which closely mirrors the corporate world, the senior pastor functions as the CEO or "point leader" of the church. The elders are not seen as fellow pastors; instead they serve as a sort of "governing board" to provide a system of checks and balances. In this system, deacons often don't exist at all. If they do, they are often seen as lower-level assistants who exist to get work done rather than as officers of the church who have New Testament authority and responsibility.

The weakness of this model is that it trades a biblical framework for a corporate one. Alexander Strauch observes, "the contemporary, church-board concept of eldership is irreconcilably at odds with the New Testament definition of eldership."[1] A church's elders should be pastors who know and care for the flock, not managers who merely govern the organization. And deacons and elders should work closely together to help the church flourish.

To identify these models as flawed is not to say that God doesn't work through them! Thankfully, he does. But if we're going to practice biblical church leadership, we need to be committed to reforming our ministry practices to bring them in line with Scripture. The fact that the Holy Spirit can work through faulty models of church leadership does not mean we should replicate those models. Jesus is the head of the church. And Jesus has taught us how he wants his church to be led. Our job is to follow his blueprint.

Let's think, then, about how the offices of elder and deacon work together in the New Testament model.

UNDER AND ALONGSIDE

First, deacons work *under* the elders, yet *alongside* the elders. Both aspects are crucial.

The office of elder/pastor is foundational in the church. Elders are the leaders charged with the preaching and teaching of Scripture

(1 Timothy 3:2; 5:17) and instruction in sound doctrine (Titus 1:9). Since the ministry of the Word is central to the church (2 Timothy 4:2), a qualified pastor is needed in every church.

Furthermore, only the elders are charged with the task of "shepherding the flock" (1 Peter 5:2). This calling mirrors the vocation of Jesus Christ, who is called the Shepherd of Israel (Psalm 80:1) and the church's Chief Shepherd (1 Peter 5:4). As under-shepherds, elders minister the care of Jesus to his people. By contrast, deacons are never called shepherds, nor are they tasked with the responsibility of shepherding the flock. Their calling is to serve.

It makes sense, then, that the office of deacon is secondary to the office of elder. Secondary does not mean unimportant! But it does involve a certain amount of deference. Deacons work ***under*** the elders. They extend the reach of the elders; they assist the work of the elders; they free the minds of the elders. Remember that in Acts 6, the apostles were tempted to "give up preaching the word of God to serve tables" (v. 2). But in order to "devote [them]selves to prayer and to the ministry of the word" (v. 4), they chose to hand off the practical care of widows. This division of labor lies at the heart of the distinction between elder and deacon. Deacons take practical concerns off the plates of the elders, so that elders can devote themselves to prayer, preaching, and shepherding.

At the same time, deacons work ***alongside*** the elders. Philippians 1:1–2 is a great picture of the unified nature of local church leadership: "Paul and Timothy, servants of Christ Jesus, To all the saints in Christ Jesus who are at Philippi, **with the overseers and deacons**: Grace to you and peace from God our Father and the Lord Jesus Christ."

Notice that the overseers and deacons are grouped together, implying shared leadership yet honoring differentiation of office. In the earliest post–New Testament churches, we see deacons working alongside bishops by reading Scripture during worship services, receiving the offerings, distributing the Lord's Supper, and leading public prayers.[2]

In a healthy church, there's a bond of collegiality, a "together for the gospel" sort of mindset, among elders and deacons. Elders don't carry their authority in a heavy-handed way, and deacons don't undercut or subvert that authority.

Only the gospel can create this kind of unity. Because elders and deacons are human beings, their relationships are sure to include mistakes and misunderstandings and foolishness and friction. Leading together as sinners, in a church full of fellow sinners, what else would we expect? If you're going to be a deacon, you need a big view of God's grace and a courageous willingness to pursue friendship, resolve conflict, and fight for unity.

WITHIN AND OUT FRONT

Second, deacons are *within* the church yet *out in front* of the church. On one hand, they are part of the church; on the other hand, they lead the church forward in key areas of service.

Regarding a deacon's presence *within* the church, J. Alec Motyer's comments on Philippians 1:1–2 are worth quoting at length:

> What is the relationship between leaders and led? The one word *with* provides the answer: "the saints *with* the overseers and deacons." . . . This kind of leadership has many facets. It involves realizing that leader and led share the same Christian experience: both are sinners saved by the same precious blood, always and without distinction wholly dependent on the same patient mercy of God. . . . It means that leaders see themselves first as members of the body and only then as ministers. In this way they face every situation from within the local body of Christ and not as people dropped in from outside. . . . and it involves co-equal sacrifice for the Lord and his gospel. It is the leadership of those who are content to stand among the saints as those who serve (Luke 22:27).[3]

If you're going to serve well as a deacon, you must always remember that you are first of all a sinner. You are "wholly dependent on the same patient mercy of God" as every other church member. When we are called into roles of leadership, we are often tempted toward a mindset of arrival. We're prone to carry ourselves with a subtle sense of pride. This demeanor is toxic to healthy Christian leadership. "By the grace given to me I say to everyone among you not to think of himself more highly than he ought to think," writes the apostle Paul in Romans 12:3. Humility is essential to godliness. So be watchful. Be prayerful. Never forget that you lead from within the church.

At the same time, a deacon's role is to be *out in front* of the church. Deacons lead by serving, and therefore they lead the church into serving.

A persistent danger throughout church history has been (and is) the "professionalizing" of ministry. This is the exact opposite of the New Testament vision. According to the Scriptures, every church member is to be actively involved in the work of ministry. Ephesians 4 reminds us: "And he gave the apostles, the prophets, the evangelists, the shepherds and teachers, to equip the saints for the work of ministry, for building up the body of Christ" (vv. 11–12). An unhealthy church is one where a few of the people do most of the ministry. A healthy church is one where all the people are engaged in ministry together. The role of the deacon is to be out in front, identifying needs and opportunities for the church to meet.

In our church, we describe a deacon as someone who a) bears ownership and responsibility for some area of ministry *beyond what a normal, mature church member would*, and b) is leading that area of ministry in a way that *takes the administrative and logistical burden off the elders*, freeing them for the work of shepherding. Every member of our church serves in children's ministry; but deacons lead and coordinate that ministry. Every member is part of a small group; but deacons lead and coordinate the small-group ministry. Every member is engaged in ministries of mercy to our city; but deacons lead and coordinate those efforts. Deacons are *out in front* of the church, setting the pace of servant leadership and building the structures that facilitate effective every-member ministry.

CONCLUSION

Since elders and deacons work together to help the church thrive, those who are called to these offices must have a clear sense of how they fit together. Deacons work *under* the elders, yet *alongside* the elders. Deacons are *within* the church, yet *out in front* of the church.

That means deacons must have the humility to come under the leadership of the elders, and also the confidence to courageously lead. They must have the spiritual maturity to guard their own souls, and also the relational maturity to work well on a team. This kind of character and maturity isn't forged overnight. It comes through patient, thoughtful application of the gospel to the unbelief and idolatry of each person's heart. That's the most important work you can do in preparation to serve as a deacon.

DISCUSSION QUESTIONS

1. Discuss your past experiences with authority. How does the idea of working under the leadership of elders challenge you?

2. Discuss your past experiences as a leader. How does the idea of being "out in front" of the church challenge you?

3. How does this lesson help you see your need for God's grace?

4. What further questions does this lesson raise for you?

3

EXERCISE

CHANGE PROJECT, PART 2

In this exercise, we're continuing the change project we began last time. Please refer back to Exercise 2 to refresh your memory on the struggle you identified.

Identify a **specific recent instance** that brought this struggle or weakness to light. Describe briefly what happened:

Now, answer as many of these questions as you can:

In that moment, what were you hoping to get or accomplish?

In that moment, what were you trying to keep or protect?

In that moment, what were you fearing or worrying about?

In that moment, who were you trying to please?

Based on your answers, what do you see yourself functionally believing about God and others? (Don't think about what you believe intellectually. Instead think about what's revealed by your behaviors and desires in that moment. This is what you *functionally* believe.)

Our more visible surface sins are always animated by deeper heart idols. If we're not worshipping the true God, we're chasing some sort of false god. Using the chart below,[4] what idol or idols can you identify at the root of your struggle?

What I Seek	The Price I'm Willing to Pay	My Greatest Nightmare	Others Often Feel . . .	I Often Feel . . .
Comfort *(privacy, lack of stress, freedom)*	Reduced Productivity	Stress, Demands	Hurt	Boredom
Approval *(affirmation, love, relationship)*	Less Independence	Rejection	Smothered	Cowardice
Control *(self-discipline, certainty, standards)*	Loneliness, Spontaneity	Uncertainty	Condemned	Worry
Power *(success, winning, influence)*	Burdened, Responsibility	Humiliation	Used	Anger
Pleasure *(feeling good, fun, enjoyment, escape)*	Broken relationships	Boredom, Feeling Trapped	Ignored and/or Used	Obsessed and Guilty

Now, try putting your struggle in "gospel language."

My "functional hell"—the thing I'm trying to avoid—is:

My "functional heaven"—the existence I'm longing for—is:

My "functional Savior"—the person or thing I'm trusting in to get me what I want—is:

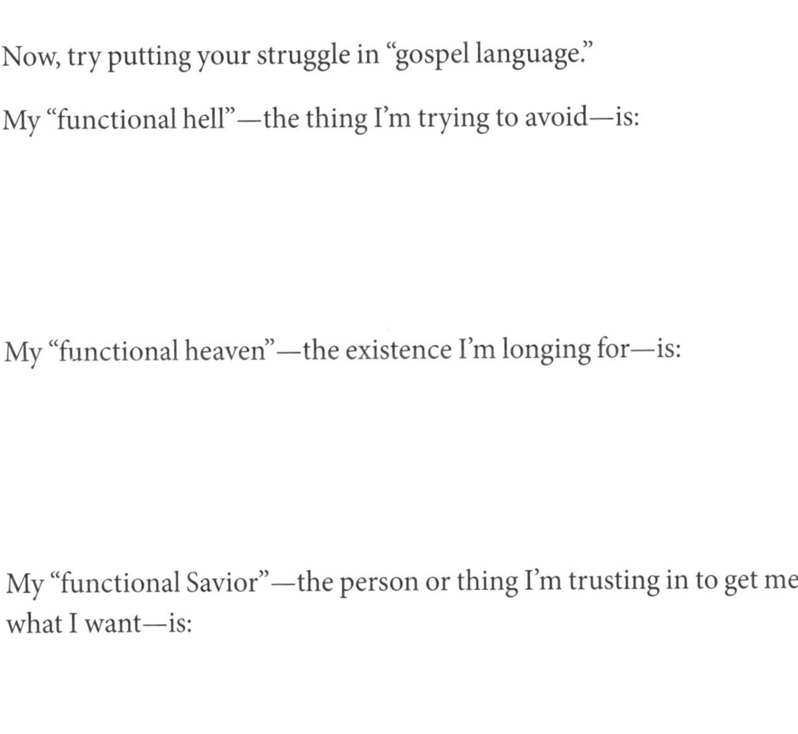

REPENTANCE

The path to change follows the steps of repentance and faith. We replace the bad fruit of sin with the good fruit of the Spirit by turning away from idols and worshipping Jesus. Below are three tangible steps of repentance.

First, turn to the Father in repentance. Name your idols to God in prayer. Here are some suggested words:

Father, I confess that I have worshipped the idol of_______. I have served it instead of serving you. I have looked to it to give me what only you can give me. And yet this false god is powerless to deliver what it promises! You alone are God, and my hope is found only in you. Forgive me for my sin and foolishness. Thank you for sending your Son to die in my place and to deliver me from all my idols.

Second, turn to the Son in worship. Acknowledge how much better Jesus is. Here are some suggested words:

Jesus, I turn to you in worship. You are better than this false Savior. It has not done for me what you have done. It has not loved me before the foundation of the world. It has not taken on flesh to redeem me. It has not died for my sin and risen victoriously over all my enemies. Forgive me for minimizing your glory and beauty. Thank you for being my merciful Savior.

Third, turn to the Holy Spirit in dependence. Acknowledge your need for his indwelling presence. Here are some suggested words:

Holy Spirit, I need you. I am weak, but you are strong. Please fill me with your presence and strengthen me by your power. Deliver me from the darkness of sin. Set me free from the enslaving power of the idols I have willingly served. Help me put to death the deeds of the flesh and walk in your light and truth.

Share your insights from this exercise with your group and rejoice together in the goodness of God. We'll continue the journey of gospel change in the next exercise.

INTERLUDE: INWARD, OUTWARD, UPWARD

In the previous three lessons, we've laid some basic biblical and theological groundwork for who deacons are. We're ready now to think more deeply about what deacons do. As I've considered the teaching of Scripture and the witness of history, I've landed on a directional metaphor for capturing the responsibilities of a deacon. Deacons face ***in***, ***out***, and ***up.*** They have an ***inward*** responsibility (toward the church family); an ***outward*** responsibility (toward the world); and an ***upward*** responsibility (toward God).

Existing resources on deacons tend to frame the duties of deacons rather narrowly. Tim Keller highlights deacons as those who "coordinate the church's ministry of mercy."[1] Rodney Stark asserts that the primary role of the deacons in the early church was "the support of the sick, infirm, poor, and disabled."[2] Alexander Strauch "speaks of the work of deacons almost entirely in terms of caring for the poor and needy within the church."[3] Thabiti Anyabwile envisions deacons as "shock absorbers" who "preserved the unity and witness of the saints."[4] The problem with viewing the role of deacons too restrictively is well stated by Bobby Jamieson in an online journal article:

> What happens in a contemporary church in which there are many more time-consuming administrative matters than distributing food to poor members? . . . Can deacons be put in charge of sound systems and child care? If not, what protects the elders' ability to devote themselves to the Word and prayer? . . . If the office of deacon was born (or at least foreshadowed) when a need arose that saddled the Apostles with too much administrative responsibility, it seems best to view

> deacons as servants who should handle all such administrative matters, rather than simply as "ministers of mercy."[5]

Additionally, by focusing primarily on the ***inward*** and ***outward*** responsibilities of deacons, modern authors risk minimizing their ***upward*** responsibility. Deacons are important guardians of a church's culture. As those charged to "hold the mystery of the faith with a clear conscience" (1 Timothy 3:9), they should be spiritual leaders within the church, holding a sound grasp of gospel doctrine and a joyful concern to see Christ glorified. They should be zealous to see "everyone mature in Christ" (Colossians 1:28). And they should be earnest worshippers, delighting in what Christ has done for ***them*** through his death and resurrection. If we focus so much on the ***practical*** responsibilities of deacons that we neglect their ***doxological*** responsibilities, we risk leading churches that get a lot done but with little love for Christ. And how foreign to the spirit of the New Testament that would be!

Let's move forward in our study, then, by considering the inward, outward, and upward responsibilities of a deacon.

4

LESSON

THE INWARD RESPONSIBILITIES OF DEACONS

OBJECTIVE

To better understand the duties of a deacon toward the church family.

SCRIPTURE READING

- 1 Timothy 5:1–25

ARTICLE

First and 2 Timothy and Titus are called the "Pastoral Epistles" because they are written to young pastors. These books are full of wisdom and direction for those who lead the church. One of the things they reveal is the responsibility church leaders have to those within the church family.

First Timothy 5:9 begins with the phrase "Let a widow be enrolled if . . ." Other translations speak of a widow being "put on the list" (NIV) or "placed on the official support list" (HCSB). In other words: this text is speaking of widows the church is responsible to support. In the first century, there were no social programs, no life insurance policies, no government safety net. Those who were vulnerable were taken care of by the church. And the New Testament church kept a list to clarify exactly who qualified. If a widow had family, her family was to take care of her; if she was younger and of marriageable age, the community around her was to help her find a spouse; only if she was at least sixty years old (1 Timothy 5:9) and had a reputation for good works was she to be added to the church's list.

Reading this passage in light of Acts 6:1–6, we can surmise that taking care of Christian widows (and others in need) was a primary task of deacons. The early church had a responsibility to those within her bounds, and that responsibility involved providing food, shelter, and material assistance. The mention of an "official support list" implies order and organization. Someone had to create the list, keep it current, and evaluate widows according to its criteria. This was the work of the earliest deacons. The fourth-century Christian document known as the Apostolic Constitutions mandates that deacons "be doers of good works, exercising a general supervision day or night, neither scorning the poor nor respecting the person of the rich; they must ascertain who are in distress and not exclude them from a share in the church funds, compelling also the well-to-do to put money aside for good works."[1]

So deacons have an inward-facing responsibility: they help care for the church family. While the inward responsibility of elders primarily relates to ***spiritual*** care, the inward responsibility of deacons relates mainly to ***practical*** care. At the risk of oversimplifying: the elders care for the spiritual needs of the flock, and the deacons assist the elders by caring for the more practical and material needs of the flock.

Of course, those needs aren't quite so easily separated. A human being is a psychosomatic unity: body and soul. Our material needs often overlap with spiritual ones, and our spiritual maladies often manifest themselves materially. Which is why we must go back to the "alongside" language of the previous chapter: deacons minister alongside elders to meet the needs of the flock. Or, as Jamie Dunlop puts it: "Elders lead ministry, deacons facilitate ministry, the congregation does ministry."[2]

A few concrete examples may help clarify how this works.

Recently, a young man in our church died of cancer. He left behind a wife and a two-year-old son. As immigrants from central Asia, they faced language and cultural barriers as they dealt with the complexities of medical care. As the sad possibility of death drew near, members, elders, and deacons in our church sprang into action.

Church members coordinated childcare, advocated for the family with healthcare professionals, and provided meals through seasons of hospitalization and chemotherapy. Elders visited in the hospital, prayed for healing, read Scripture aloud with the couple, and eventually officiated the funeral. They also counseled members of the church about walking through death and grief by faith. After the funeral, a deacon was dispatched to sit at the kitchen table with the grieving widow and review all her financial obligations. He then brought her needs before a broader group of deacons, who disbursed funds from the church's treasury to help pay funeral expenses and bills. Throughout the whole process, a spirit of partnership was evident. Sometimes a pastor or elder was leading the charge. Other times, a deacon took the lead. And in other cases, a church member would reach out with a call to action. The full range of local church ministry was on display as members, deacons, and elders each fulfilled their biblical responsibility.

A second example: as our church has grown, we've discerned an increased need for biblical counseling among our church members. There was a time when we could meet the demand by making a pastor available as needed. But we've outgrown that capacity. Now, a team of deacons and elders works together to provide biblical counseling to our church community.

One of the pastors on our team oversees the care and counseling ministry, ensuring that it's faithful to Scripture and in line with our theological convictions. He also oversees the training and equipping of counselors, and does much biblical counseling himself, often stepping into the most difficult or complicated situations. Three deacons—one man and two women—work alongside him. They "extend his reach" by meeting with church members themselves. One of these deacons plays the role of point person: when someone reaches out for biblical counseling, he connects with them and walks them through an intake process and schedules them for a meeting. He also prepares briefings for the elders to help them keep a pulse on the ministry, since biblical counseling is a subset of the church's broader shepherding work. As these deacons and elders work together, people grow in Christ and the body builds itself up in love (Ephesians 4:16).

These examples are only two vignettes of how deacons fulfill their inward responsibilities, working alongside elders and members. If you're going to "serve well" as a deacon (1 Timothy 3:13), you must be responsive to the needs of God's people. You must be attentive to the particular places within your local church where better organization will lead to more effective ministry. Where's the "official support list" in your church? Who's keeping it current? Who's making sure it gets executed? Who's making sure no one gets overlooked (Acts 6:1)?

Often, pastors and church members ***are*** aware of the needs within the body; it's just that no one is organizing, systematizing, and executing the meeting of those needs. That's what deacons do. They bring order where there's disorder, clarity where there's confusion, and structure where there isn't any. They make serving easier. They create pathways for people to get involved in ministry. They find solutions to the problems that hinder the church's care for her members.

This brings us back to the point made in the Introduction: *deacons are doers*. They are proactive, not reactive. No one should take the title of deacon merely because they want a position, or because they want to be seen as a leader. Deacons make things happen. They take initiative, they identify needs, they move toward problems. One of my pastor friends, in appointing a new deacon to oversee an area of ministry, told her: "Your job is to take this area of ministry off my mind." It wasn't that he was unwilling to invest time and energy in that area of ministry; in fact, he'd been doing it for years! Rather, he wanted her to understand her freedom and responsibility and agency as a deacon. As she gave leadership to that aspect of the church's ministry, she was freeing her pastor to *not* think about it. And in a growing ministry, that's a great blessing.

CONCLUSION

As you anticipate the various ways you will fulfill your inward responsibilities, remember the bigger picture: your Father in heaven is meeting the needs of his people through you. Jesus told his disciples: "Do not be anxious, saying, 'What shall we eat?' or 'What shall we drink?' or 'What shall we wear?' For the Gentiles seek after all these things, and your heavenly Father knows that you need them all. But seek first the kingdom of God and his righteousness, and all these things will be added to you" (Matthew 6:31–33). If we ask *how* our heavenly Father will meet these needs, part of the answer is: through the local church! God gives his church deacons, and charges them to "serve well" (1 Timothy 3:13), so that through them his people can experience his fatherly care.

Let that sink in: our Father in heaven is manifesting his love for his people through you. May that fill you with joy, and worship, and gratitude as you respond to the needs in ***your*** church.

DISCUSSION QUESTIONS

1. Why do you think the early church had a list of widows? What does this teach us about the spiritual importance of order and organization?

2. What do you think about the apostles' criteria for who should make the list? How is this instructive for us today?

3. Where do you see your own church doing a good job fulfilling its inward responsibilities? Where might there be room for growth?

4. What further questions does this lesson raise for you?

4

EXERCISE

CHANGE PROJECT, PART 3

In this exercise, we're continuing the change project we've been working on. Please refer back to Exercises 2 and 3 to refresh your memory on the "bad fruit" you've identified.

The path to change follows the steps of repentance and faith. We concluded Exercise 3 by focusing on repentance. In this exercise, we want to focus on faith. All of our sins are rooted in unbelief. If we always lived with full confidence in God as our Creator, Redeemer, Lord, and King, we'd never disobey him or turn away from him.

Repentance and faith aren't really two separate steps; they're more like two sides of the same coin. To repent is to turn back to God, trusting his promises and counting his Word as true. Faith is expressed in **believing truth** (instead of lies) and **worshipping God** (instead of idols). So let's go back to the "bad fruit" you've identified—and the specific situation in which you saw it play out—and let's ask the following questions.

What would **"good fruit"** look like in your area of struggle? Describe how your particular episode might have gone differently if you were growing in expressing the fruit of the Spirit (Galatians 5:22–24).

What would **replacing lies with truth** look like in your area of struggle? Identify which of the following truths—or another biblical truth not listed here—you are failing to believe. What would it look like to "put this truth to work" in your moment of struggle?

- Creation: This is my Father's world, and everything in it is to be used for his glory (1 Corinthians 8:6).
- Lordship: God is the Lord, and he is to be the supreme authority in my life (Romans 13:14).
- Incarnation: God became human in Jesus, entering into my world and drawing near to me (John 1:14).
- Redemption: Jesus bought me with a price and brought me to himself (1 Corinthians 6:19–20).
- Adoption: Through Jesus, I belong to God and he belongs to me (Galatians 4:4–7).
- Sanctification: The Holy Spirit now lives in me, and I have the power to change (Ephesians 3:16).

What would **purposeful worship** look like in your area of struggle?

- Daily, personal worship: Does your daily practice show that you can't live without the Word of God? How do your prayers relate to your particular area of struggle?

- Weekly, corporate worship: What might need to change about how you engage with God and his people on Sundays?

What would **renewed obedience** look like in your particular area of struggle?

- What practices or habits provoke your particular sinful desires? (Think in terms of particular situations, media, people, activities, times of day, etc.)

- What do you need to "put off" (Ephesians 4:22)?

- What practices or habits stir your affections for Christ and his people? What do you need to "put on" (Ephesians 4:24)?

Now, pause and express faith in God through prayer. Confess your unbelief. Talk to him about your desire to embrace his promises again. Ask the Holy Spirit to fill you with fresh faith and empower you for renewed obedience.

5

LESSON

THE OUTWARD RESPONSIBILITIES OF DEACONS

OBJECTIVE

To better understand the duties of a deacon toward those outside the church.

SCRIPTURE READING

- Leviticus 19:9–18

ARTICLE

The Christian message begins with mercy. "At one time we too were foolish, disobedient, deceived and enslaved by all kinds of passions and pleasures. We lived in malice and envy, being hated and hating one another. But when the kindness and love of God our Savior appeared, he saved us, not because of righteous things we had done, but *because of his mercy*" (Titus 3:3–5 NIV). In gratitude for God's mercy, Christians are to act mercifully toward others. And deacons are the church's designated ministers of mercy.

Mercy can be defined as the "impulse that makes us sensitive to hurts and lacks in others and makes us desire to alleviate them."[1] The early church saw mercy ministry as a gospel imperative (Acts 11:28–30; Romans 12:13). And they understood that needy Christians should be the church's first concern. "As we have opportunity, let us do good to everyone, and ***especially*** to those who are of the household of faith" (Galatians 6:10).

Tim Keller notes that this "especially" clause is rooted in the Old Testament principle of covenant:

> The ministry of mercy was primarily a *covenantal* blessing. That is, it was a healing ministry for those who entered into God's covenant by promising to live under God's kingship. . . . The Old Testament social legislation included mercy to strangers, but the laws for giving to the poor favored the fellow Israelite. . . . The closer the covenantal connection, the greater the responsibility for mercy.[2]

So mercy ***begins*** within God's covenant family: the Israelite gets first priority. But the church's mercy also ***extends*** to the poor outside the church. Just as the Old Testament law made provision for the stranger and the sojourner in Israel (e.g., Leviticus 19:9–10, 33–34), the church is sent on mission to spread the kingdom of God to outsiders.

> To spread the kingdom of God is more than simply winning people to Christ. It is also working for the healing of persons, families, relationships, and nations; it is doing deeds of mercy and seeking justice. It is ordering lives and relationships and institutions and communities according to God's authority to bring in the blessedness of the kingdom.[3]

By heeding Scripture's call to show mercy to outsiders, Christians in the Roman Empire made God's invisible kingdom visible. During a plague in AD 251, Bishop Dionysius of Alexandria contrasted the crass response of the pagans with the cheerful self-sacrifice of the Christians:

> At the first onset of the disease, [the pagans] pushed the sufferers away and fled from their dearest, throwing them into the roads before they were dead and treated unburied corpses as dirt, hoping thereby to avert the spread and contagion of

> the fatal disease. . . . Most of our brothers [i.e., the Christians] showed unbounded love and loyalty, never sparing themselves and thinking only of others. Heedless of danger, they took charge of the sick, attending to their every need and ministering to them in Christ—and with them departed this life serenely happy; for they were infected by others with the disease, drawing on themselves the sickness of their neighbors and cheerfully accepting their pains.[4]

A century later, the Roman emperor Julian the Apostate lamented that his own attempts to re-paganize the empire were being thwarted by the indiscriminate mercy of the "impious Galileans":

> These impious Galileans not only feed their own poor, but ours also; welcoming them into their agape, they attract them, as children are attracted, with cakes. Whilst the pagan priests neglect the poor, the hated Galileans devote themselves to works of charity. . . . See their love-feasts and their tables spread for the indigent. Such practice is common among them and causes a contempt for our gods.[5]

The mercy shown by Christians was one of the primary reasons for the growth of Christianity in the Roman world. Likewise, in a skeptical, post-Christian age like ours, meeting the needs of outsiders plays a key role in the church's missionary witness. "The mercy ministry of Christians provides tremendous social and psychological support for the validity of the gospel. . . . It convinces a community that *this* church provides people with action for their problems, not only talk. It shows the community that *this* church is compassionate."[6]

MERCY IN PRACTICE

Deacons take the lead in moving the church outward to address the needs of its community. What does this look like in practice? Here are a few guiding principles.

Get to know your neighborhood

Many churches are ingrown. They aren't attuned to the needs of their community, and their members don't have meaningful relationships with non-Christians. If your church is prone toward an inward focus, the first step is humble repentance and faith. Start by confessing your own personal self-absorption. Then gather a few other people and invite them to do the same. Repentance spreads. Humility is attractive. Before you know it, your church may start to experience renewal!

Then, do the work of getting to know your actual neighbors. Learn their needs and longings, their hopes and fears. You can't gain this sort of knowledge online. You can only gain it in person. And you'll be surprised how ministry opportunities rise to the surface once you start talking to people.

A few years ago, our church purchased a building and moved to a new address. We'd been renting space nearby for a decade; but we hadn't been a stakeholder in the neighborhood. Once we purchased a highly visible property on a major street, we knew the neighbors would be curious about our presence. We decided to take the opportunity to do an in-depth study of the community.

One deacon and five volunteers led the research project, which included personal interviews with over four dozen local leaders, observational visits to local parks and community centers, and door-to-door surveys in ten surrounding neighborhoods.[7] By talking to hundreds of neighbors, we were able to discern the major mercy ministry needs that our church was equipped to meet. We also built great rapport in the community. Neighbors were surprised to meet "church people" who were going door-to-door to learn rather than to proselytize. And over the past few years, we've executed a simple mercy ministry plan that's borne good fruit and given us further opportunities to proclaim the gospel.

Identify existing ministries before starting new ones

Years ago, I served on staff in a campus ministry that had over fifty "departments"—all doing mostly the same thing. Why? Because the organization would let its staff launch almost any new initiative—as long as they could raise money for it. Churches and city-focused ministries are prone to a similar sort of inefficiency. We often fail to explore whether someone else is already doing the thing we feel motivated to do.

Faithful deacons steward the church's resources well by learning what's already going on in the city. What ministries already exist? What non-profits are doing similar work? Who else is trying to solve similar problems?

In leading our own church, we discovered that many of our members were motivated toward pro-life causes: reducing abortions, helping at-risk mothers, encouraging foster care and adoption. One of our deacons identified a half-dozen ministries in our city that were already working in these areas, from pregnancy resource centers to Christian adoption agencies to safe houses for victims of sex trafficking. Rather than starting our own ministries, we chose to mobilize our church to get involved in the good work these groups were already doing. As an added benefit, we've built strong intra church relationships through serving side-by-side with other Christians.

Start with what you're already doing

It's likely that the members of your church are already engaged with various ministries in your community. Not all these ministries will be suitable for the church as a whole to engage in, but some may be.

A long-standing member of our church served for years as a chaplain at the local prison. Over the course of time, she developed relationships with hundreds of formerly incarcerated women. She noticed that their biggest struggles took place not while they were in prison, but as they entered back into destructive patterns and relationships upon their release. She felt prompted by the Holy Spirit to start a post-incarceration ministry to help women make wise decisions and build healthy life patterns. What began as a small Bible study has blossomed into a growing ministry serving almost a hundred women each week.

As the ministry began, our elders and deacons simply offered prayer and encouragement. We've found it wise, as Jesus counseled, to ensure people are "faithful in little" (Luke 16:10) before entrusting them with broader resources. As the ministry grew and bore good fruit, the church's deacons began to provide organizational support, coaching, and funding. Eventually, one deacon took primary responsibility, mobilizing the church body to support the ministry through volunteering, financial giving, and providing rides and meals. Now this ministry, started by one faithful church member, is one of our church's main mercy initiatives.

CONCLUSION

After the apostles appointed the seven "proto-deacons" in Acts 6, we read that "the word of God continued to increase, and the number of the disciples multiplied greatly in Jerusalem, and a great many of the priests became obedient to the faith" (Acts 6:7). Wouldn't it be great to see the word of God "continue to increase" in your city? Wouldn't you love to see the number of disciples multiply greatly? Wouldn't it be wonderful to see more and more people become obedient to the faith? These things happen, in part, as deacons fulfill their outward responsibilities. As neighbors see God's people meeting needs in the community and serving those outside the church, social and psychological barriers to the gospel are diminished. Even those who begrudge our actions will have to admit, as did Julian the Apostate, that Christians "devote themselves to works of charity."

So what are the barriers to mercy in your own heart? Who do you see as "deserving" of help? Who do you see as undeserving? How do you feel about the needy people in your neighborhood? Where do you lack the heart of Jesus toward the distressed and downtrodden? Pause now and invite the Spirit of God to search your heart and show you what you need to see. Remember where you were when the mercy of God found you (Titus 3:3–5). Then turn to Christ for fresh courage and faith to move out in mercy toward outsiders.

DISCUSSION QUESTIONS

1. "The closer the covenantal connection, the greater the responsibility for mercy." What do you think about this principle? What might it mean for mercy ministry in your church?

2. How much of your understanding of your neighborhood or community is based on actual conversations with people who live and work there? What could you do to become more attuned to the needs around you?

3. What have you been convicted or challenged about as you've read this lesson?

4. What further questions does this lesson raise for you?

5
EXERCISE

CHANGE PROJECT, PART 4

In this exercise, we're continuing the change project we've been working on. Please refer back to Exercises 2, 3, and 4 to refresh your memory on the "bad fruit" you've identified and the repentance and faith connected to it.

In the previous exercises, we've looked backward. After identifying some area of sin or weakness in your life, you focused on a specific recent example that brought this struggle or weakness to light. Like an athlete watching "game tape" of a recent competition, the goal was to look back at a moment in the past and consider what could have been different.

In this exercise, we want to look forward. We want to anticipate the next moment where this struggle is prone to arise. Like an athlete watching film of an upcoming opponent, we want to strategize how to proactively respond in a "game time" situation.

First Corinthians 10:13–14 says:

> No temptation has overtaken you that is not common to man. God is faithful, and he will not let you be tempted beyond your ability, but with the temptation he will also provide the way of escape, that you may be able to endure it. Therefore, my beloved, flee from idolatry.

This exercise is intended to help you anticipate a future moment of temptation, and see the "way of escape," so that you may more intentionally flee from idolatry.

Think back to this question you answered in Lesson 2 (add any new insights you may have gained over the past few weeks): *WHEN do you struggle the most with this "bad fruit"? What specific situations or circumstances tend to bring it to the forefront?*

Now, anticipate: In the next few weeks, when might you find yourself in a similar circumstance or situation?

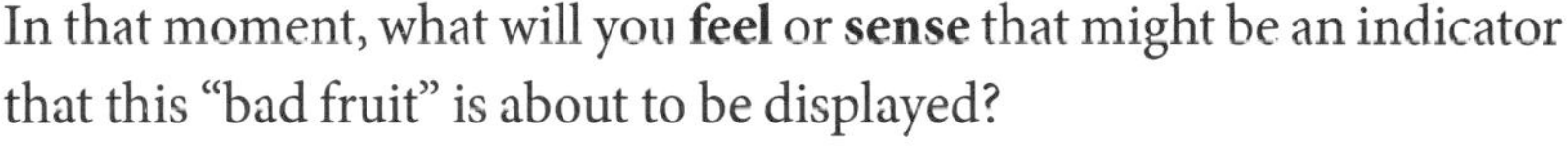

In that moment, what will you **feel** or **sense** that might be an indicator that this "bad fruit" is about to be displayed?

Pause and pray now. Ask the Holy Spirit to make you soft and attentive **in that future moment** to the warning signs you've identified.

Take a moment to visualize the future situation you anticipate. Where might you be standing? Is anyone there with you, or are you alone? What time of day is it? What are your surroundings?

Imagine yourself, in that moment, ***choosing*** to worship Jesus Christ. What new actions or responses can you envision flowing out of that decision? What "good fruit" do you see coming forth?

Pause and pray now. Worship Jesus that he died not only for your past sins, but for your future ones as well. Ask the Holy Spirit to fill your heart with worship in that future moment of struggle. Then, by faith, expect him to meet you in that moment!

6
LESSON

THE UPWARD RESPONSIBILITIES OF DEACONS

OBJECTIVE

To better understand the worship focus/responsibilities of deacons.

SCRIPTURE READING

- Psalm 63

ARTICLE

The great danger of what we've said so far about deacons is that it all sounds very pragmatic. Deacons are doers. Deacons are servant leaders. Deacons help care for the church family and minister to the needs of the community. It's possible to focus on these practical aspects of ministry and miss the most important responsibility of a deacon: worship. Deacons help lead a church toward a deeper pursuit of God.

After all, if deacons *merely* attend to practical needs, then what's distinctly Christian about their work? Many non-profits and humanitarian aid agencies do similar things. A deacon who's hard-hearted toward God, immature in faith, or shallow in biblical wisdom could still execute the functions of the role. But because deacons share the responsibility to "make disciples of all nations" (Matthew 28:19) and "present everyone mature in Christ" (Colossians 1:28) and "give an account" for the souls of God's people (Hebrews 13:17), they must be alive with love for God and for his church. Their most important responsibility is an upward responsibility: pointing people to the glory of God in Christ.

As visible leaders within a church, deacons, along with the elders, are pacesetters. They help to set the tone for what's normal, expected, and commended. If elders and deacons are satisfied with tepid worship, perfunctory prayers, and weak evangelism, then that's what the church will have. But if the elders and deacons are hungry for more of God; if they long for earnest and prevailing prayer; if they're zealous to see non-Christians come to faith; then the church will be marked by that kind of spirit. As the wise old saying goes, "more is caught than taught." We learn implicitly from our surroundings. We observe the example of others, and we follow in their footsteps. Their practices become ours.

In the mid–twentieth century, Hungarian-born scientist and philosopher Michael Polanyi developed the theory of *tacit knowledge*. His contention is that "we know more than we can tell." Human beings are capable of knowledge that goes beyond our ability to rationally explain. We can recognize a familiar face in a sea of faces. But why? We can't really explain this sort of knowledge; yet it is true knowledge. A pianist "knows" how to play the piano; but when she plays, she's unconscious of what her fingers are doing. She looks at the music on the page, and her fingers just know what to do.[1]

Likewise, the people in your church "know" what's expected, what's normal, what's commendable. They know this because they take cues from the church's visible leaders. So how do you help your church know God more deeply? By seeking that knowledge yourself! In order to lead a church toward deeper pursuit of God, deacons must be hungry for God themselves. That might sound a bit abstract, so to help you, here are three practical action steps.

CULTIVATE PERSONAL COMMUNION WITH GOD

One of the most powerful insights I've gained from the Puritans is the distinction between *union* and *communion*. Understanding the difference opens up a whole new world of confidence, joy, and growth in grace. Kelly Kapic explains:

> Believers are *united* to Christ in God by the Spirit. This union is a *unilateral action* by God, in which those who were dead are made alive, those who lived in darkness begin to see the light, and those who were enslaved to sin are set free to be loved and to love. . . . the human person is merely receptive, being the object of God's gracious action.
>
> Communion with God, however, is distinct from union. [To experience it, we must] *respond* to God's loving embrace. While union with Christ is something that does not ebb and flow, one's experience of communion with Christ can fluctuate . . . prayer, corporate worship, and biblical meditation . . . tend to foster the beautiful experience of communion with God. Giving in to temptations and neglecting devotion to God threaten the communion, but not the union.[2]

A Christian's union with Christ is unilateral and secure. It's a settled fact. But our communion with God, as Kapic points out, does ebb and flow. And it can be strengthened by discipline and weakened by neglect. Church leaders must help God's people *rest in their union with Christ* and *strive for communion with Christ*. And to do so, we must lead by example.

So: What strengthens your devotion? What fans the flame of communion with God for you? What spiritual practices awaken in you a deeper love for God, and help you feel a deeper sense of his love for you?

Probably, these questions would be answered by you partly based on your individual temperament. But the basic means of grace—prayer, corporate worship, Scripture reading, and the sacraments—are the primary means of communion with God for every Christian. As a deacon, you must make it a priority to be diligent in both private and public means of grace. And it's important to view these practices not as ends in themselves, but as a means of communing worshipfully with the triune God.

INTEND UNIVERSAL OBEDIENCE

It's disheartening to realize how many Christian leaders have been disqualified through personal sin and indiscretion. Holiness is an urgent need in the church. How can we foster holiness? And how can we grow in our own personal holiness? John Owen in his famous treatise *On the Mortification of Sin* answers this question by urging Christians to "intend universal obedience." Owen wrote *Mortification* in 1656 because he wanted to help Christians *actually* conquer sin and live in holiness. In a message that is still relevant 350 years later, Owen reminds us that it's possible to conquer sin. God promises as much in Romans 8:13: "If by the Spirit you put to death the deeds of the body, you will live."

The problem is that many Christians don't actually ***intend universal obedience***—that is, they haven't resolved to obey God in ***every*** area. "He that would really, thoroughly, and acceptably mortify any [sin] must take care to be equally diligent in all parts of obedience," Owen writes. "It is not only an intense opposition to this or that peculiar lust, but a universal humble frame and temper of heart, with watchfulness over every evil and for the performance of every duty, that is accepted."[3] Owen's scriptural grounding for this observation is 2 Corinthians 7:1, where Paul urges the Christians at Corinth: "Cleanse yourselves from ***all*** pollution of the flesh and spirit, perfecting holiness in the fear of God."

As I reflect on Owen's counsel, I'm struck by how well he understands the human soul. I'm often attentive to some particular area of sin that's troubling to me while ignoring broader areas of obedience that matter equally to God! I make peace with small areas of sin and selfishness, content that I'm working on the bigger areas that "really matter." Owen reminds me that ***intending universal obedience*** is the only path to holiness. In his estimation, a struggle with one particular sin is "commonly the fruit and issue of a careless, negligent course in general."[4]

What about you? Where have you been careless or negligent in your obedience to God? Have you submitted to the Lord Jesus fully and wholeheartedly, and are you ***actively*** seeking to obey him in every area? Are there parts of your life you're holding back; are there secrets from your past you haven't brought into the light; are there hidden sins you're cherishing?

Perhaps the thought of "intending universal obedience" is overwhelming to you and you feel paralyzed by the enormity of the task. But thankfully the gospel of Jesus Christ is not only the way into the Christian life, it's the way forward in our Christian life. We don't conquer sin alone. We do it by going to God and every day asking for forgiveness for our many sins, accepting God's forgiveness, and asking for the Spirit of God to fill us with the life of Christ. This is the life all Christians are called to—one of daily repentance where we turn from our sin and turn in faith to Jesus.

PRACTICE LIFESTYLE REPENTANCE

In 1517, Martin Luther sparked reformation and renewal in the church by inviting church leaders to publicly debate 95 propositions. The statements he posted have become known to history as Luther's 95 Theses. The very first thesis reads: "Our Lord and Master Jesus Christ, when He said "Repent" (Mt. 4:17), willed that the whole life of believers should be repentance."[5]

In Luther's day, repentance had become confused with penance. Most people "repented" by confessing their sins to a priest and then performing whatever penitential penalties the priest prescribed. This led to an external religiosity that bypassed the heart and made repentance into a work. This mechanistic view of repentance persists today. When most of us hear the word "repent," we think of something weighty, decisive, and dramatic. But as Luther put it, "the whole life of believers should be repentance." Repentance is something we do every day. It's the ongoing turning of the heart back to God (Joel 2:12–13). It's ongoing awareness of our heart idols and unbelief (Hebrews 3:12–13). It's the consistent invitation for God to "search [us] and know [our] hearts" by his Spirit (Psalm 139:23).

When's the last time you remember repenting before the Lord in prayer? Was it as recent as today, or has it been awhile? Are you aware right now, in this moment, of your need for God's grace?

One reason most of us don't repent more frequently is because we tend to be focused on sins of *commission*—things we do that actively disobey God. But the Bible also focuses on sins of *omission*—our failures to honor and serve God as we should. The Westminster Shorter Catechism defines sin this way: "Sin is any want of conformity unto, or transgression of, the law of God" (WSC 14). "Transgression" is the catechism's word for sins of *commission*. "Want of conformity" identifies sins of *omission*. When we transgress God's law, we should repent. And when we fail to conform to God's will in any way, we should repent.

So: Are you repenting of the weakness of your love toward God? Or the tepidness of your worship last Sunday? Or your tendency to rely on your own strength rather than the Holy Spirit? Once your eyes are open to the "want of conformity to the law of God" in your own life, you should find plenty to repent of!

In light of the gospel, repentance is always a joy, never a burden. Our Father has adopted us into his family by grace, and he's committed to transforming us into the image of his Son. So he sends forth the Spirit to do the work of conviction. Awareness of sin is the Father's invitation to turn toward him in repentance, to believe the good news of the gospel by faith, and to submit to the ongoing work of his Spirit in our lives.

CONCLUSION

"A rising tide lifts all boats," says an old proverb. Deacons and elders set the "spiritual tide" of a local church. As their spiritual expectations are raised, the energy and vitality of the whole church increases. That's why deacons must not neglect their upward responsibilities. Though their work from day to day and week to week may be quite practical and hands-on, faithful deacons must diligently cultivate communion with God. They must intend universal obedience to the Lord Jesus Christ. And they must practice ongoing repentance.

So how are you doing currently in these areas? Where do you need change, growth, or renewed diligence? Reflect on your present reality using the questions below. Then discuss your observations with a group or mentor.

DISCUSSION QUESTIONS

1. What's your current experience of communion with God like?

2. Have you resolved to obey God in ***every*** area? Where do you notice negligence or carelessness in your pursuit of holiness?

3. What are you currently repenting of? What new insights about repentance were sparked through this lesson?

4. What further questions does this lesson raise for you?

6

EXERCISE

PRACTICING COMMUNION WITH GOD

This exercise will help you evaluate your current spiritual practices; identify needed areas of growth; and explore how a right view of grace can deepen and strengthen your fellowship with God.

So let's start by reflecting on your current practices. Imagine someone spent an entire week alongside you: doing what you do, going where you go.

What would that person's experience of **prayer** be like? In what situations would they see you praying? How often? Would they come away sensing that prayer is an important part of your life? Write about it.

What would that person's experience of **Scripture** be like? How and when would they see you reading, studying, hearing, or meditating on Scripture? Would they conclude that the Bible is an important part of your week? Write about it.

What would that person's experience of **conversation** be like? Would they hear you speak of God normally and naturally? Would Jesus be a regular subject of conversation at home, at work, over meals, or with friends? Would anything in your speech shock, offend, or trouble them? Write about it.

What would that person's experience of your **priorities** be like? Would they sense that your life is oriented around the local church? Would they see you prioritizing evangelism and discipleship? Would they see you sharing the gospel with someone, or praying with someone, or giving biblical counsel to someone? Write about it.

What strengths and good habits does this exercise reveal?

What gaps and weaknesses does this exercise reveal?

The gospel is the good news that you are accepted before God based on Jesus's death and resurrection, not your works. He doesn't love you more because of your diligence in spiritual practices, and he doesn't love you less because of your flagging and faltering discipline.

How does God's steadfast love for you in Jesus, despite your weakness, awaken you to renewed resolve?

How can you bring your weaknesses before your Father in heaven? What do you need to ask for and receive from him?

What new commitments do you need in order to cultivate consistent communion with God? Who will you ask for prayer, encouragement, and accountability?

7
LESSON

THE PECULIAR TEMPTATIONS OF LEADERSHIP

OBJECTIVE

To consider some peculiar dangers and temptations that leaders face.

SCRIPTURE READING

- 1 Samuel 15; 2 Samuel 11–12

  Pay attention to how both Saul and David use their position of authority as an "excuse" to disobey God.

ARTICLE

Every Christian understands the reality of temptation. So does Jesus, of course: "We do not have a high priest who is unable to sympathize with our weaknesses, but one who in every respect has been tempted as we are, yet without sin" (Hebrews 4:15). But what we often fail to realize is that temptation is situational.

That's what makes ***temptation*** different from ***fantasy***. Fantasy operates in a dream world. You may fantasize about scoring a touchdown in the Super Bowl, being one of the first humans to live on Mars, or stealing top-secret government secrets from the Chinese. But you are not *tempted* to do any of these things. Temptation operates in the world of the possible. We are tempted by things we actually *could* do.

Which is why stepping into an office of leadership in the local church awakens new kinds of temptation. You will now have opportunities to sin in ways that are peculiar to leadership. For instance: you can use your authority in heavy-handed and ungodly ways (see Mark 10:42–43 and 1 Peter 5:3). You can become proud, using your position as a badge of identity and worth (see 1 Timothy 3:6). You can steal money from the church coffers or use church resources for personal gain (see John 12:6). Though the character traits manifested in these sins won't be new, the opportunity to express them will be. So let's consider five specific seductions that leaders often face.

The seduction of entitlement. A position of authority always brings with it the danger of entitlement. Entitlement says "I shouldn't have to do X" or "I have a right to Y." It could be as simple as "I'm entitled to a good parking spot," or as complex as "I have a right to be respected by others." Entitlement always reflects a subtle works-righteousness: "Since I've done *this*, God owes me *that*." Rather than being awed by the gospel of grace and humbled by the opportunity to serve Christ, entitled people are focused on their own merits and desires.

Reflection Question: What do you feel entitled to?

The seduction of comfort. A life of leadership in the church is a life of sacrifice. But for many of us who have been raised in a prosperous culture, sacrifice is not a welcome idea. Leaders are perpetually tempted by the allure of comfort. This can take many forms: the comfort of a generous budget, the comfort of a predictable schedule, the comfort of not having to minister in ways you find difficult or challenging. The inclination toward comfort often manifests itself in a desire to control the demands leadership places upon us: How much time will this take? What will it demand of me? How can I fit it into my already existing schedule? If you find yourself asking these questions, you may need to examine where comfort has a grip on your soul.

Reflection Question: What comforts do you resist giving up for the sake of serving Christ?

The seduction of pleasure (or escape). Whether it's a growing ministry, a disgruntled church member, or a broken and needy neighbor, deacons are perpetually immersed in challenging situations. The temptation to escape is strong. When leaders are not resting in the presence, promises, and provision of the Lord Jesus Christ, they will be prone to seek a "quick fix" in sex, food, gambling, entertainment, alcohol, or some other momentary pleasure. Those who have had victory over lust for years may find themselves suddenly tempted by pornography. Those who live very disciplined lives may be suddenly tempted by laziness and apathy. Often the temptation toward pleasure goes hand-in-hand with entitlement: "Since I've been working so hard in ministry, I deserve this little indulgence."

Reflection Question: Where do you go when you want to escape?

The seduction of greed. Scripture requires deacons who are "not greedy for dishonest gain." But the character vice of greed takes many forms. Among leaders, greed often shows up as *a relentless drive for more*—more people, more money, a growing ministry, a bigger platform, a wider influence. Christians sometimes baptize this sort of greed as a longing for "kingdom growth." But underneath, it's often driven by ego and a thirst for reputation.

Reflection Question: Where do you see in yourself a relentless drive for more?

The seduction of affirmation. People tend to look up to, respect, and admire their leaders. And this approval and affirmation is inherently seductive. All of us enjoy being liked! If deacons are not deeply grounded in God's approval of them, they can begin to find identity in people's approval of them. Their ministry becomes about pleasing people rather than pleasing God. They find themselves adapting to people's preferences and devastated by criticism or conflict.

Reflection Question: Whose affirmation (or lack thereof) has the greatest effect on you?

Perhaps, after reflecting on these five seductions, you're starting to doubt whether you have what it takes. Who wouldn't be seduced by these things? How can you persist in ministry for the long haul without giving in to these temptations?

The grace of the Lord Jesus Christ is the answer. All five of these seductions are rooted in self-glory, self-righteousness, and self-sufficiency. So the way to defeat them is to allow our hearts to rest deeply in the glory, righteousness, and sufficiency of the Lord Jesus.

Jesus is the truly glorious one. He is the one my heart truly longs for—the beauty my soul was made to embrace. The temporary, fleeting satisfactions of pleasure, comfort, affirmation, and ministry growth simply do not and will not fulfill my deepest longings. Their glory pales in comparison to Jesus.

Jesus has given his righteousness to me. My righteousness counts for nothing—all my righteous deeds are like filthy rags (Isaiah 64:6). I come bankrupt to Jesus and am clothed with his righteousness by grace through faith. Therefore, I have no "rights" to demand. I "deserve" nothing. Everything is grace. I'm not entitled to anything, nor do I lack anything, because I am in him (Philippians 3:7–11). I rest in his righteousness when things go well, and I rest in his righteousness when things go poorly.

Jesus is sufficient for all my needs. If I have Jesus, I am rich, though I lack everything else (Philippians 3:8). I need nothing to complete me or make me whole; because of the love of Christ, I am filled with all the fullness of God (Ephesians 3:19). I can be content in seasons of great comfort, affirmation, and ministry success, and I can be content in seasons of suffering and hardship and difficulty—because in every season, I have Christ, and he is sufficient (Philippians 4:11–13).

It's one thing to believe these truths about Jesus. It's another thing to revisit them over and over again until they sink in deeply and begin to affect the fundamental "operating system" of our hearts. A life of gospel ministry is a life of constant communion with Jesus—constantly returning to this good news over and over again. As we believe this good news and let it "get down deep" into our souls, we find that the power of the gospel increasingly frees us to resist the peculiar temptations of leadership.

DISCUSSION QUESTIONS

1. Have you ever thought about leadership bringing with it its own set of temptations? How should that change the way you approach leadership?

2. Which of the five seductions (entitlement, comfort, pleasure/escape, greed, affirmation) is most alluring to you personally? Why?

3. "It's one thing to believe these truths about Jesus. It's another thing to revisit them over and over again until they sink in deeply." How will you keep these truths fresh in your mind and heart?

4. What further questions does this lesson raise for you?

7

EXERCISE

IDENTIFYING YOUR TEMPTATIONS

Author and counselor Paul David Tripp, in his book *Dangerous Calling*, observes: "All of us have the tendency in our sin to become very skilled self-swindlers. . . . If you aren't daily admitting to yourself that you are a mess and in daily and rather desperate need for forgiving and transforming grace . . . you are going to give yourself to the work of convincing yourself that you are okay."[1]

The goal of this exercise, then, is to prevent "self-swindling" by helping you grow in self-awareness, specifically in identifying your vulnerability to these five seductions. With that, let's revisit the five reflection questions in the article.

1. What do you feel entitled to?
2. What comforts do you resist giving up for the sake of serving Christ?
3. Where do you go when you want to escape?
4. Where do you see in yourself a relentless drive for more?
5. Whose affirmation (or lack thereof) has the greatest effect on you?

Based on your answers, pick one of the five seductions to really focus on. Though all of them may tempt you at various times, there's probably one that you're particularly vulnerable to, based on your story or your personality.

What specific shape might this seduction take in your *actual* ministry? (What comforts or pleasures would you be prone to seek? If you wanted "more" of something, what would it be? Whose affirmation would you be influenced by?) Answer as specifically as you can.

Tripp later goes on to say in *Dangerous Calling*:

> It is only worship of Christ that has the power to protect [us] from all the seductive idols of ministry that will whisper in [our] ears. It is only the glory of the risen Christ that will guard [us] against the self-glory that is a temptation to all who are in ministry. . . . It is only a heart that is satisfied in Christ that can be spiritually content in the hardships of ministry.[2]

Write a paragraph here about the glories of Christ—specifically, how Jesus is better than the seductions you face. What truths about Jesus most move your heart? What aspects of his person and work are most compelling to you?

8

LESSON

THE LEADERSHIP JOURNEY

OBJECTIVE

To understand church leadership not as a destination, but as a journey toward deeper fellowship with Jesus.

SCRIPTURE READING

- 2 Timothy 4:1–8

ARTICLE

Being a deacon is not a destination.

It's important that you know that. Otherwise, you'll treat it as a goal to be reached instead of a stewardship to be exercised. If God is calling you toward leadership in the church, he doesn't just want to work *through* you; he wants to work *in* you. His plan is to sanctify you through leadership.

> Consider it all joy, my brethren, when you encounter various trials, knowing that the testing of your faith produces endurance. And let endurance have its perfect result, so that you may be perfect and complete, lacking in nothing. But if any of you lacks wisdom, let him ask of God, who gives to all generously and without reproach, and it will be given to him. (James 1:2–5 NASB95)

Rest assured that ministry will be full of trials. Difficult people, challenging seasons of ministry, church conflict, and demonic opposition will take a toll on the faithful deacon. Leaders are often tempted to see these trials as problems to be solved, obstacles to be overcome, challenges to be met. But God's goal in these trials and tribulations is the formation of your character. He is making you into a certain kind of person. As E. M. Bounds expressed it, "The church is looking for better methods; God is looking for better men"[1] (and we can add "better women" too).

In other words, serving as a deacon will be both *functional* and *formative*. It will be *functional* in the sense that your work as a deacon should be effective, productive, and helpful to the mission of the church. It will be *formative* because serving as a deacon is one of God's means to shape your soul and grow you as a disciple of Jesus Christ.

Colossians 1:6 (NASB95) tells us that the gospel is "continually bearing fruit and growing" in us. All of life is a context for gospel growth. For those of us who lead others, this means that our leadership isn't only about presenting others "mature in Christ" (Colossians 1:28)—it's about growing in our own Christlikeness as well. Deacons who see their office as a destination are at high risk of becoming prideful, stagnant, and ineffective. But those who see it as an opportunity for formation are likely to remain humble, teachable, and soft toward the Spirit's work.

Let's consider a few aspects of the leadership journey that are crucial both to the effective *functioning* of the diaconal office and to the spiritual *formation* of the people who serve in that office.

LEADERSHIP COMES WITH EXPECTATIONS

As one of the primary preaching pastors in our church, I preach thirty to forty Sundays each year. And because that's part of my responsibility, our church members show up on Sundays *expecting* me to have a sermon ready! That's not an unrealistic expectation; it's a right expectation. It's commensurate with my role and responsibility.

Likewise, your work as a deacon will come with certain expectations. You are stepping into a visible role of leadership in the church. You are taking responsibility for some area of ministry. You should expect people to have expectations of you, and you should welcome those expectations.

Expectations are *functional* because they help us get things done. I must have a sermon prepared by Sunday morning each week; it's what my job requires and what God's people (rightly) demand. Sometimes a sermon comes together smoothly. But sometimes I'm banging my head against a wall on Thursday afternoon or losing sleep on Saturday evening. Either way, the consistent expectation of a weekly sermon keeps me steadfast and diligent in my work.

Expectations are *formative* because they force us to grow. Sometimes, the expectations people have are unrealistic, and I have to gently tell them so. Other times, the (right) expectations that come with my role as a pastor require me to trust God, grow in competence, manage my time better, admit my limitations, delegate to others, or learn a new skill. All of these things are formative: they demand personal growth and transformation.

If you are asked to step into the office of deacon, be sure you understand the expectations of the role. What are you being asked to do? How will you know if you're doing it well? What goals should you aim for? What are the marks of success or effectiveness? Then, ask the Holy Spirit to use these expectations as a means of formation in your life. Acknowledge your need, lean on his strength, and embrace the opportunity to become more like Jesus.

Reflection Question: How do you distinguish realistic expectations from unrealistic ones?

LEADERSHIP IS ABOUT PRESENCE

Edwin Friedman, a Jewish rabbi and family therapist who died in 1996, observed that the relational dynamics of a congregation are similar to those of a family. Effective leadership in either setting requires the ability to discern and navigate relational systems. Poor leaders display *a failure of nerve*: they lack the courage to stand firm in the midst of other people's emotional reactivity.[2]

Friedman asserts that leadership is really about *presence*. A leader's job is to be a peaceful presence—to be "the strength in the system." Rather than taking on the anxiety and reactivity of the emotional system around them, good leaders transform that anxiety by their calm, steady, well-differentiated presence.

If you're going to lead in the local church, you're going to come up against "anxious system" dynamics: reactivity, herding, blame-shifting, a quick-fix mentality. Wise leadership is going to require you to swim upstream *against* this anxiety rather than getting caught up in it.

Cultivating a "non-anxious presence" is *functional* because it calms anxiety and defuses reactivity. People don't make good decisions or relate well to others when they're agitated. Leaders who are able to enter into conflict, listen without defensiveness or judgment, and then bring wise and thoughtful solutions are a gift to the church. They embody the peaceful presence of Jesus. They bring steady, calm leadership to volatile moments. And they stand gently but firmly against those who would hijack the mission of the church or disrupt its unity and peace.

Cultivating a non-anxious presence is *formative* because it requires deep personal transformation. Most of us can be calm and steady in our best moments. But what about when you're slandered by a church member? Or when your small group erupts in conflict and disagreement? Or when handful of vocal people want the pastor fired? Or when a marriage is in turmoil and the whole church is taking sides? Staying differentiated in moments like these requires a strong sense of self, deep fellowship with God, mature wisdom, and settled confidence in God's promises. These qualities don't "come naturally." They are forged intentionally over time. As Dallas Willard put it: we must train "off the spot" to build the virtues and habits that matter when we're "on the spot."[3]

Reflection Question: Describe an anxious or reactive situation you've been in recently. What did you learn from the experience?

LEADERSHIP HAS SEASONS

Once you step into a role of leadership, you're likely not going to hold it for life! You'll probably serve in this role for a season, and then hand it off to someone else. Perhaps your church has terms of office that require such a handoff; and even if it doesn't, it's still a good practice! Churches that aren't consistently raising up new leaders tend to become stagnant and ingrown.

For a church to maintain a vibrant ministry, leaders must die to themselves. Each deacon must have an accurate perception of his or her strengths and limitations. And he or she must recognize that deacon is an office, not an identity. A person can be *deacon-qualified* without serving in the office of deacon. My vision for every leader in our church is for them to be raising up and training someone to replace them. This is what the apostles did. It's what every subsequent generation has done. And it's an excellent way to keep a church healthy and vibrant.

A person who makes a good deacon in a church of one hundred may not be such a good deacon in a church of one thousand. As a church or movement grows, different types of competence and skill are required. Good deacons think of themselves "with sober judgment" (Romans 12:3). They understand that in some seasons they may be a perfect fit, and in other seasons another leader may need to take over.

Similarly, deacons may go through seasons of life where they are not able to devote the time and energy necessary to serve the church well. A person who has a health crisis in the family, or who is raising a special-needs child, or is asked to take on a new level of responsibility at work may not be able to function in the office of deacon at the capacity the church needs. In these moments, the humility to step out of the office and entrust the work to others is a crucial gift to the church.

Deacons must recognize the seasonal nature of leadership. They must be willing to humbly step aside if circumstances require it, or if the needs of the church outpace their giftedness or ability. This is *functional* because it adjusts to the changing nature of ministry. It is *formative* because it builds humility and selflessness that younger leaders can see and emulate. A church full of people who qualify as deacons, have served for a season, and have handed the baton to others is a refreshing anomaly in a world driven by pride, power, and position.

Reflection Question: How will you hold the office of deacon with open hands, offering yourself to the Lord and to his work without clinging to title or position?

CONCLUSION

Leadership is a journey, not a destination. Serving as a deacon provides a powerful opportunity for God to shape your soul and grow you as a disciple of Jesus Christ. So remember: as you minister to others, the Holy Spirit is also doing his work in you. Attend to his work. Welcome it. And thank him for it. "I am sure of this, that he who began a good work in you will bring it to completion at the day of Jesus Christ" (Philippians 1:6).

DISCUSSION QUESTIONS

1. Expectations, Presence, Seasons—which of these ideas was most helpful for you, and why?

2. What most excites you about the possibility of serving as a deacon?

3. What do you find most intimidating or faith-stretching about the possibility of serving as a deacon?

4. What further questions does this lesson raise for you?

CONCLUSION

Congratulations! You've reached the end of this study. It's my prayer that the Holy Spirit has used it to both encourage and challenge you in your pursuit of leadership. If you've made it to this point, you've taken in a lot of information. But don't mistake information for transformation.

To further the Spirit's work of transformation, it will be helpful as you conclude this study to spend time in prayer and reflection. Invite the Holy Spirit to confirm some specific, tangible areas where you need further growth and development.

Vision: As you've progressed through this study, what one or two things have you been most challenged or convicted about by the Holy Spirit?

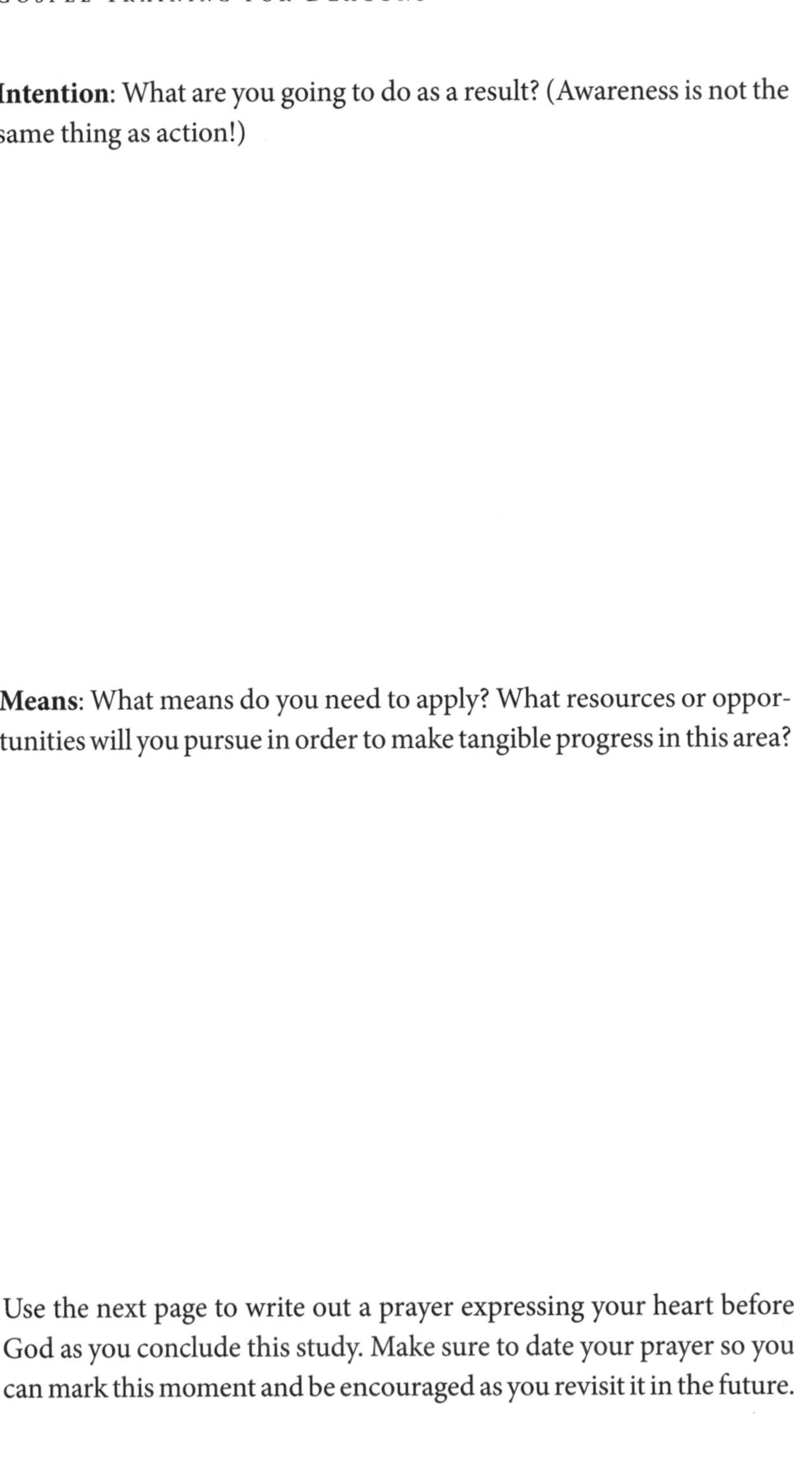

Intention: What are you going to do as a result? (Awareness is not the same thing as action!)

Means: What means do you need to apply? What resources or opportunities will you pursue in order to make tangible progress in this area?

Use the next page to write out a prayer expressing your heart before God as you conclude this study. Make sure to date your prayer so you can mark this moment and be encouraged as you revisit it in the future.

ENDNOTES

Introduction: What Is a Deacon?

1. Alfons Weiser, "*diakoneo*," *Exegetical Dictionary of the New Testament*, ed. Horst Balz and Gerhard Schneider, vol. 1 (Grand Rapids: Eerdmans, 1990), 302.

2. "A distinction may be made between all these general uses and the employment of the term as the 'fixed designation for the bearer of a specific office . . .'" Hermann W. Beyer, "*diakonos*," *Theological Dictionary of the New Testament*, ed. Gerhard Kittel, trans. Geoffrey W. Bromiley, vol. 2 (Grand Rapids: Eerdmans, 1964), 89.

3. Ralph Martin, *Philippians*, Tyndale New Testament Commentaries (Grand Rapids: Eerdmans, 1959), 57–58.

4. Alec Motyer, *The Message of Philippians*, BST Commentary Series (Downers Grove, IL: InterVarsity Press, 1984), 25 (emphasis added).

5. William D. Mounce, *Pastoral Epistles*, Word Biblical Commentary, vol. 46 (Nashville: Thomas Nelson, 2000), 163.

6. However, I can't conclude that installing deacons before elders would be unbiblical, especially in a church-planting context. The apostles clearly installed elders as the first step in establishing a self-governing church (see Acts 14:23 and Titus 1:5, in particular); but Scripture does not command a particular order.

7. Some of the scriptural duties of an elder include: prayer and the ministry of the word (Acts 6:4); ruling/leading the church (1 Timothy 5:17); managing the church (1 Timothy 3:4–5); caring for people in the church (1 Peter 5:2–5); being godly examples (Hebrews 13:7); rightly using the authority God has given them (Acts 20:28); teaching the Bible correctly (Ephesians 4:11; 1 Timothy 3:2); preaching (1 Timothy 5:17); praying for the sick (James 5:13–15); teaching sound doctrine and refuting false teachers (Titus 1:9); disciplining unrepentant Christians (Matthew 18:15–17).

8. Thomas Oden and Peter Gorday, *Ancient Christian Commentary on Scripture*, New Testament vol. 9 (Downers Grove: InterVarsity, 2000), 175.

9. Will Walker and Kendal Haug, *Providence Deacon Training*, unpublished manuscript, 2019. Obtained through personal correspondence with the authors.

Lesson 1: Servant Leadership

1. Serge, *Sonship*, 3rd ed. (Greensboro, NC: New Growth Press, 2013), 1–2.

Lesson 2: Biblical Qualifications for Deacons

1. Hermann W. Beyer, "diakonos," *Theological Dictionary of the New Testament*, ed. Gerhard Kittel, trans. Geoffrey W. Bromiley, vol. 2 (Grand Rapids: Eerdmans, 1964), 89.

2. Thomas Oden and Peter Gorday, *Ancient Christian Commentary on Scripture*, New Testament vol. 9 (Downers Grove: InterVarsity, 2000), 175.

3. F. L. Cross and E. A. Livingstone, eds., *The Oxford Dictionary of the Christian Church*, 3rd ed. Revised (Oxford University Press, 2005), "deaconess," 459.

Lesson 3: Deacons and Elders

1. Alexander Strauch, *Biblical Eldership* (Colorado Springs: Lewis and Roth, 1995), 16.

2. See F. L. Cross and E. A. Livingstone, eds., *The Oxford Dictionary of the Christian Church*, 3rd ed. Revised (New York: Oxford University Press, 2005), "deacon," 458.

3. J. A. Motyer, *The Message of Philippians*, BST Commentary Series (Downers Grove, IL: IVP Academic, 1984), 27–28.

4. This chart is adapted from Darrin Patrick, *Church Planter* (Wheaton, IL: Crossway, 2010), 162–67. In a footnote, Patrick acknowledges that he's building upon the work of Dick Kaufman (in unpublished lectures) and Dick Keyes (in the book *No God but*

God: Breaking with the Idols of Our Age, ed. Os Guiness and John Seel [Chicago: Moody Press, 1992]).

Interlude: Inward, Outward, Upward

1. Timothy J. Keller, *Ministries of Mercy: The Call of the Jericho Road*, 2nd ed. (Phillipsburg, NJ: P&R Publishing, 1997), 42.

2. Rodney Stark, *The Triumph of Christianity: How the Jesus Movement Became the World's Largest Religion* (New York: HarperCollins, 2011), 114.

3. Bobby Jamieson, "Book Review: The New Testament Deacon: the Church's Minister of Mercy, by Alexander Strauch," 9 Marks Journal, April 30, 2010, https://www.9marks.org/review/new-testament-deacon-churchs-minister-mercy-alexander-strauch/.

4. Thabiti Anyabwile, *Finding Faithful Elders and Deacons* (Wheaton, IL: Crossway, 2012), 21.

5. Jamieson, "Book Review: The New Testament Deacon."

Lesson 4: The Inward Responsibilities of Deacons

1. Quoted in Rodney Stark, *The Triumph of Christianity: How the Jesus Movement Became the World's Largest Religion* (New York: HarperCollins, 2011), 114.

2. Jamie Dunlop, "Deacons: Shock-Absorbers and Servants," 9 Marks Journal, March 31, 2010, https://www.9marks.org/article/deacons-shock-absorbers-and-servants/.

Lesson 5: The Outward Responsibilities of Deacons

1. Timothy J. Keller, *Ministries of Mercy: The Call of the Jericho Road*, 2nd ed. (Phillipsburg, NJ: P&R Publishing, 1997), 46.

2. Keller, *Ministries of Mercy*, 81.

3. Keller, 84, 54.

4. Quoted in Rodney Stark, *The Triumph of Christianity: How the Jesus Movement Became the World's Largest Religion* (New York: HarperOne, 2011), 115–17. Stark's endnotes indicate that the original source is Eusebius, *The History of the Church* 7.22.

5. "Julian the Apostate - New World Encyclopedia," accessed December 23, 2023, http://www.newworldencyclopedia.org/entry/Julian_the_Apostate. Quoted from Charles Schmidt, *The Social Results of Early Christianity* (London: Wm. Isbister, 1998), 328, and Gaetano Baluffi and Denis Gargan, *The Charity of the Church, a Proof of Her Divinity* (Dublin: M.H. Gill and Son, 1885), 16.

6. Keller, *Ministries of Mercy*, 212.

7. The tool we used was the Neighborhood 360 assessment from Seed to Oaks (https://seedtooaks.com/).

Lesson 6: The Upward Responsibilities of Deacons

1. See Michael Polanyi, *The Tacit Dimension* (Chicago: University of Chicago Press, 1966).

2. Kelly Kapic, "Introduction," in John Owen, *Communion with the Triune God* (Wheaton, IL: Crossway, 2007), 21–22.

3. John Owen, *Of the Mortification of Sin in Believers*, http://www.ccel.org/ccel/owen/mort.html, accessed December 29, 2023.

4. Owen, *Of the Mortification of Sin in Believers*, Chapter VIII.

5. "Disputation of Doctor Martin Luther on the Power and Efficacy of Indulgences" (1517), https://www.projectwittenberg.org/pub/resources/text/wittenberg/luther/web/ninetyfive.html.

Lesson 7: The Peculiar Temptations of Leadership

1. Paul David Tripp, *Dangerous Calling: Confronting the Unique Challenges of Pastoral Ministry* (Wheaton, IL: Crossway, 2012), 33.

2. Tripp, *Dangerous Calling*, 64.

Lesson 8: The Leadership Journey

1. E. M. Bounds, *Power through Prayer* (Grand Rapids: Baker Book House, 2001), 11.

2. See Edwin Friedman, *A Failure of Nerve: Leadership in the Age of the Quick Fix* (New York: Church Publishing, 2007).

3. See Dallas Willard, *The Renovation of the Heart: Putting on the Character of Christ* (Colorado Springs: NavPress, 2002), 90.